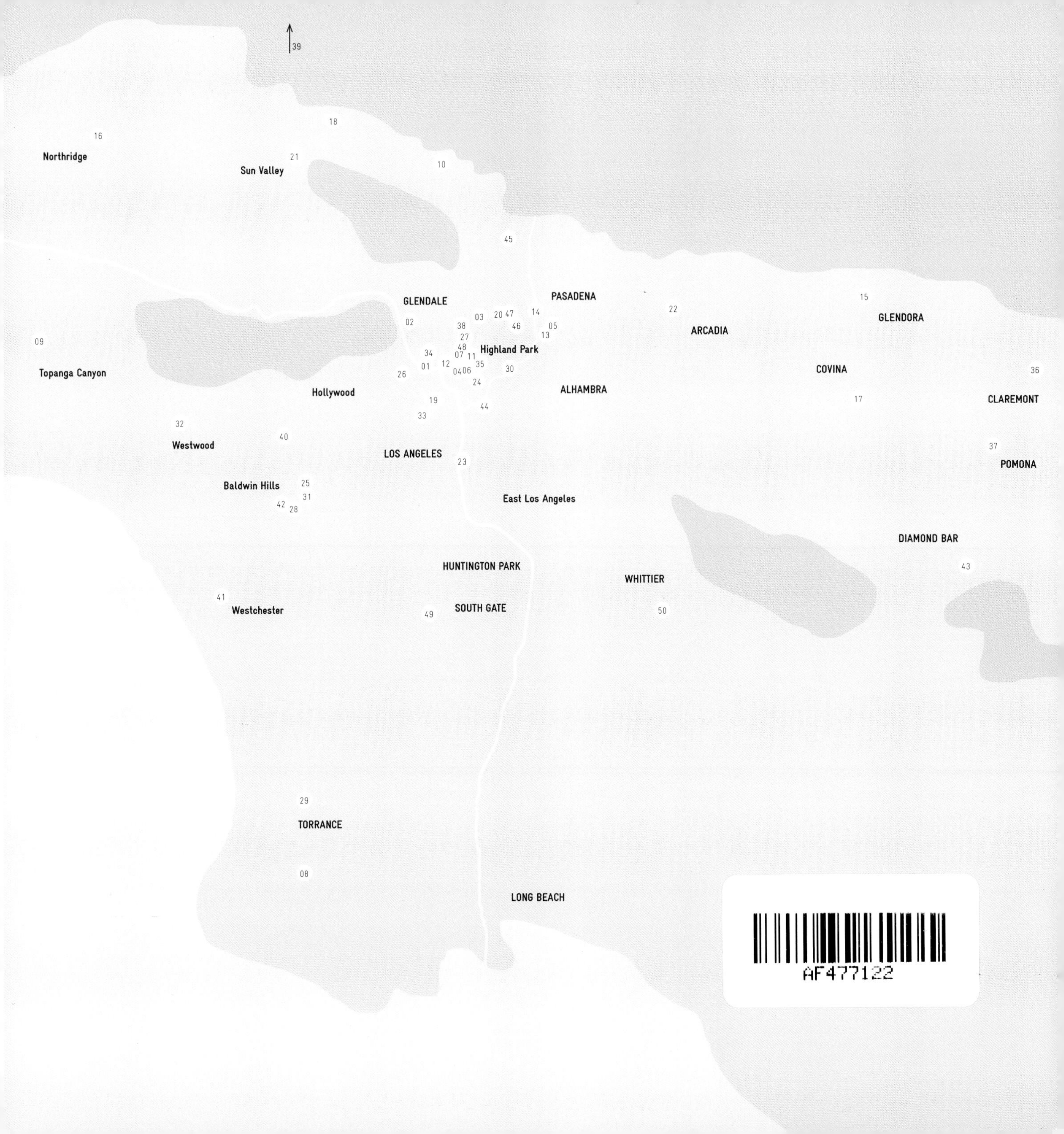

39
16
Northridge
18
Sun Valley
21
10
45
GLENDALE
PASADENA
02
03
20 47
14
38
46
05
22
ARCADIA
15
GLENDORA
27
13
09
34
48
Highland Park
07 11
COVINA
36
Topanga Canyon
01
12
35
30
26
0406
CLAREMONT
24
17
Hollywood
19
ALHAMBRA
32
33
44
40
37
Westwood
LOS ANGELES
POMONA
23
Baldwin Hills
25
31
East Los Angeles
42 28
DIAMOND BAR
41
43
Westchester
HUNTINGTON PARK
WHITTIER
49
SOUTH GATE
50
29
TORRANCE
08
LONG BEACH
AF477122

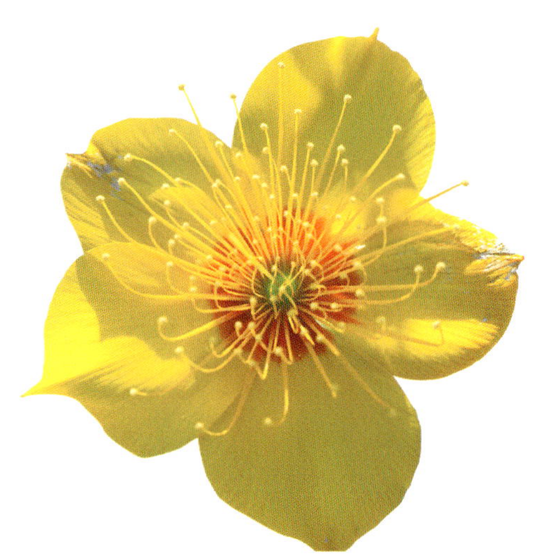

Mentzelia lindleyi (Blazing Star)

Thirsty manicured landscapes of clipped

evergreen shrubbery and lawns cover this city that supposedly
has no seasons, no sense of time, and an aversion to all evidence
of aging or death. The story of Los Angeles' native wildflowers
is more complex, nuanced, localized, and ever-changing.
Long-anticipated early winter rains germinate seeds that have
been lying in wait, buried in dry soils from the low coasts to the
high deserts, from the valley flats to the mountain slopes.
Gradual growth with cool temperatures and low sun through
winter months give way to an early spring explosion of bright
green and rainbow color. The story of the season is told with
the timing and extent of the bloom in direct proportion
to the rainfall, temperatures, and climate. The plants turn to
a crisp golden brown as the dry summer months return, and the
flowers prepare to broadcast their seeds for next year's story.

Fritz Haeg, 2013

When I first came to California [in 1893],

what impressed me perhaps more than anything else was the wonderful native flora. But as the years went by it was with deep regret that I saw the wild flowers so rapidly disappearing from the landscape. I made up my mind that I would try to do something to awaken a greater interest in the native flora. Thus it was that I began to specialize in the growing of wild flowers and native plants. I collected seed of a few kinds of wild flowers, grew them and offered the seed for sale.

Little or no success attended this first venture, it being generally conceded that it was foolish to waste time on "wild flowers." As a demonstration [in 1905] I secured the use of a vacant lot in Hollywood and sowed it with wild flower seeds. I went to Walter Raymond of the Raymond Hotel in Pasadena and asked him for the use of a piece of ground for sowing wild flower seeds. Mr. Raymond readily consented and the following spring there was a splendid display. I also secured the use of two lots in Pasadena, one on Green Street and the other at the corner of Lake and Colorado, which I sowed with wild flower seeds. All these plots were greatly admired and I received complimentary letters from many people…

While roaming around in the San Fernando Valley, I noticed
that certain areas would produce a succession of flowers
and color effects — yellow predominating at one time, blue
at another, and so on. I wondered if the same effects could
be produced artificially so I began to experiment by mixing
several kinds of seeds, sowing them and watching the results.
It was in this way that I perfected my wild flower mixtures
which have since become so popular.

Theodore Payne in 1961

from *Theodore Payne in His Own Words: A Voice for California Native Plants,* 2004

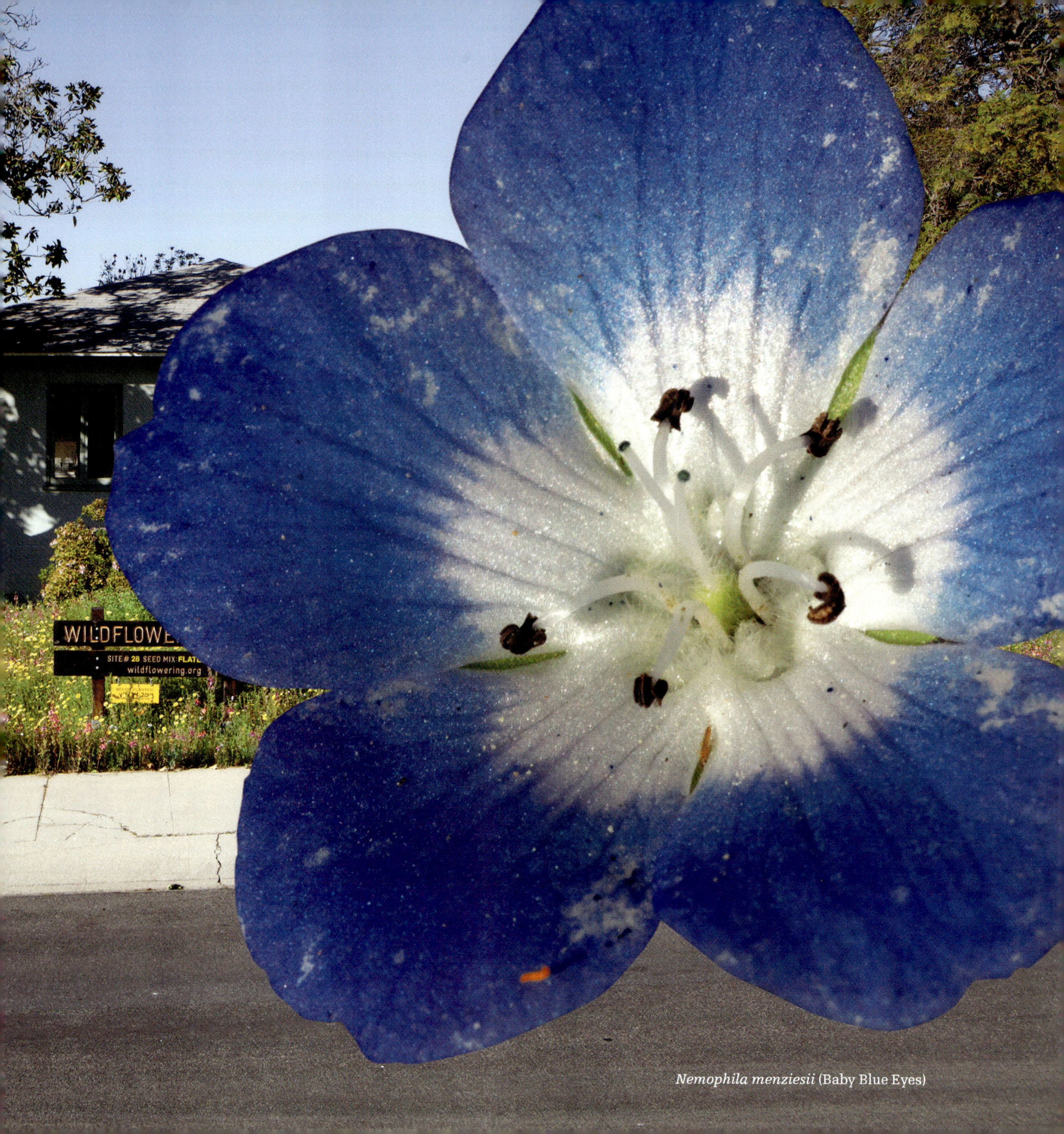

Nemophila menziesii (Baby Blue Eyes)

WILDFLOWERING L.A.

a project by Fritz Haeg

Wildflowering L.A. is a native wildflower seed sowing initiative throughout Los Angeles County by artist Fritz Haeg. Fifty highly visible sites were sown by participants in fall 2013 to bloom in spring 2014. The project included various events throughout the course of the season, and culminated with a participatory public exhibition.

Curated and presented by LAND (Los Angeles Nomadic Division),
the project brought a wild and beautiful seasonal native landscape to open plots
of land throughout Los Angeles County.
The sites were selected from an open call based on public visibility and distribution
across the county. Owners of selected sites were given free native wildflower seed mixes.
Soil preparation, seeding, and wildflower tending were demonstrated by the
Theodore Payne Foundation, and one of four custom wildflower seed mixes was
prescribed — Coastal, Flatlands, Hillside, and Roadside — inspired by
Reyner Banham's 1971 book, *Los Angeles: The Architecture of Four Ecologies*. Each of the
participating sites was officially identified with a prominent carved wood sign.

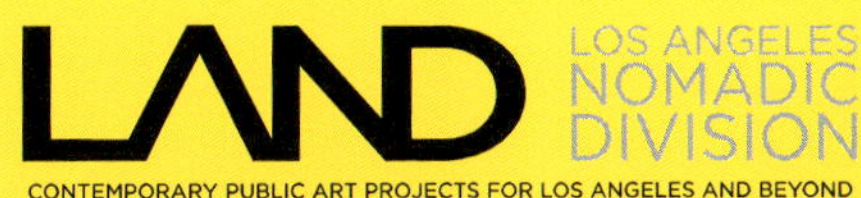

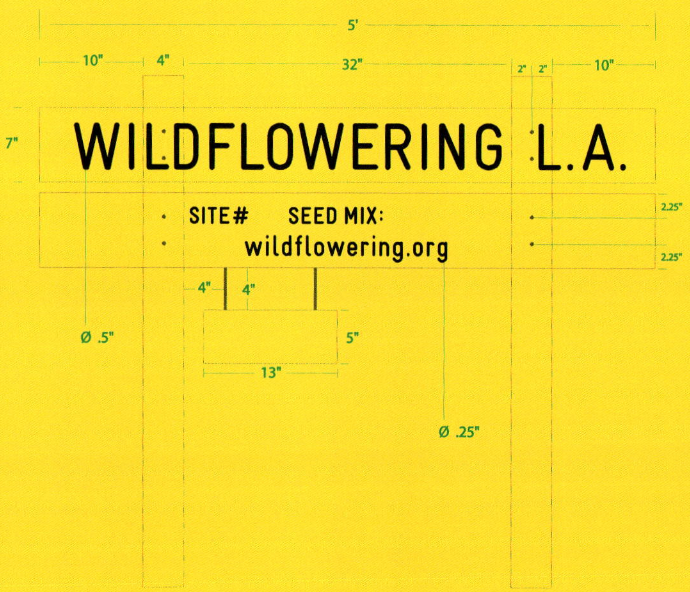
5'
10"
4"
32"
2" 2"
10"
7"
WILDFLOWERING L.A.
SITE #   SEED MIX:
wildflowering.org
2.25"
2.25"
4"
4"
Ø .5"
5"
13"
Ø .25"

TABLE OF CONTENTS

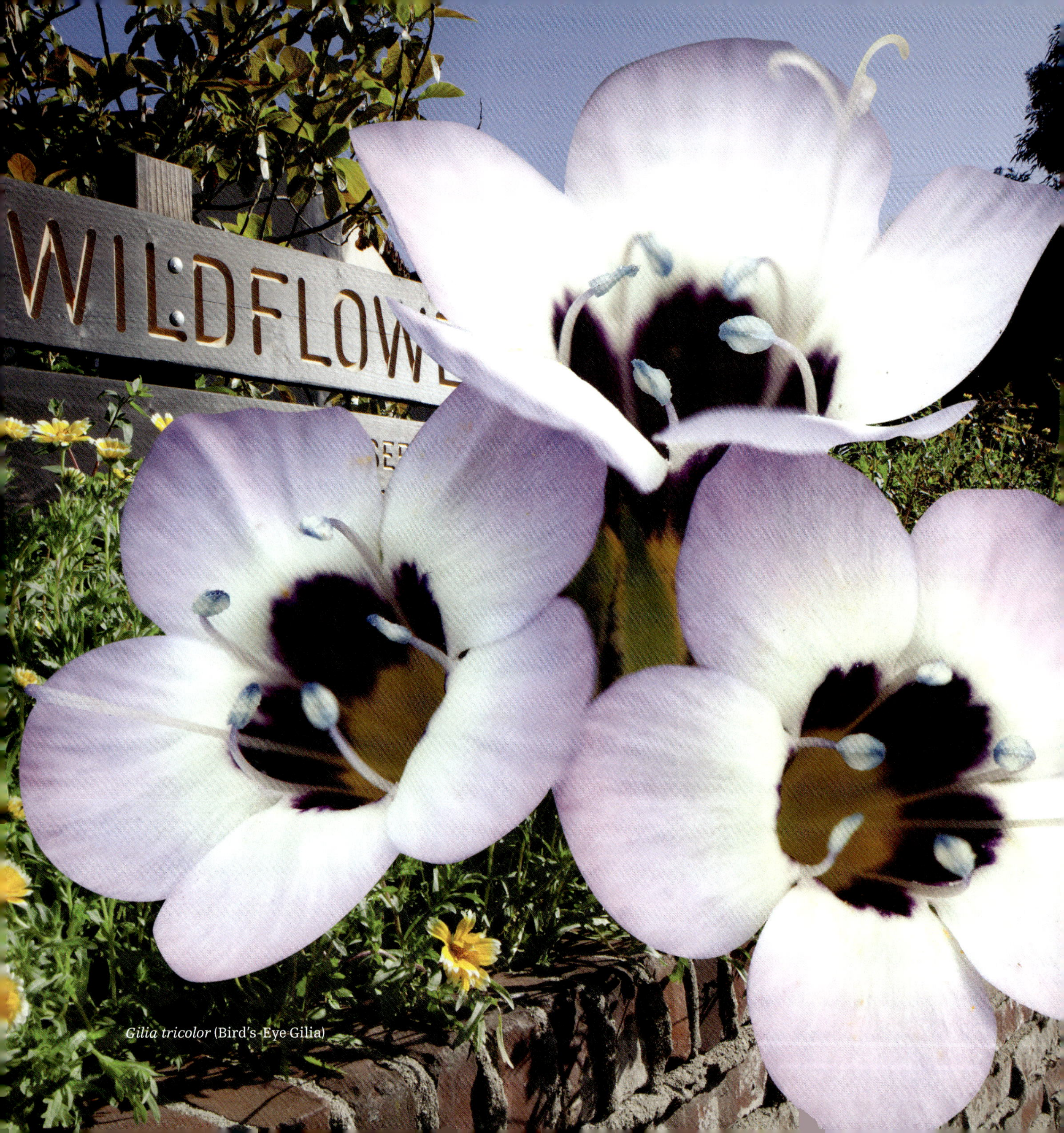

Gilia tricolor (Bird's-Eye Gilia)

Introduction

Fritz Haeg's *Wildflowering L.A.* is, to date, the most ambitious site-specific project LAND (Los Angeles Nomadic Division) has undertaken with a single artist. Embracing unpredictability as part of its own core conceit — from the vagaries of site ecologies, invasive plants, gophers, and a record-breaking drought to a reliance on mobilizing volunteers for months of ongoing labor and dedication — *Wildflowering L.A.* grew in focused bursts across 4,752 square miles of greater Los Angeles, from coastal Palos Verdes Peninsula to the semi-arid northeastern corner of Los Angeles County in the shadow of Mount Baldy. Between those two sites (South Coast Botanic Garden, Site #08 and Pitzer College, Site #36), the landscape was punctuated by fifty native wildflower meadows that bloomed from March through May 2014 at locations including school gardens, front yards, public parks, industrial street corners, traffic medians, along public stairways, and even at the entrance of a United States Post Office, as well as a full acre at the Los Angeles County Arboretum and Botanic Garden. This publication serves not only as documentation of the *Wildflowering L.A.* project, but also as a handbook of inspiration and instruction on how to grow native California wildflowers.

Haeg's artistic practice is invested in ecological history, collective production, education, evolving models for home and living, and often, the places where these considerations meet through experiments on an individual and group level. Some projects occur over a constricted time or locale, while others are of longer duration and broader geography, including *Edible Estates* (a series of public domestic edible gardens in 15 cities internationally from 2005-2014) and *Animal Estates* (a housing initiative for native wildlife, initiated in 2008).

Wildflowering L.A. harkens the utopian spirit of California in the 1960s but was reliant upon much that defines our contemporary age, from social media hashtagging to a necessary interest in native landscape restoration and municipal water conservation programs. The project simultaneously recalls two other iconic periods in the psychogeography of southern California: Theodore Payne's attempts at preserving the disappearing native wildflower landscape in the 1890s and park signage of the Works Progress Administration era in the 1930s (with a design update by Roman Jaster and produced in Los Angeles by the Knowhow Shop). At each site, *Wildflowering L.A.* created nodes that were seemingly wild and yet highly constructed.

The Theodore Payne Foundation for Wild Flowers and Native Plants was a fitting consultant for the project, given the organization's mission, history, and knowledge of native California wildflower growing methods and local microecologies. Seed sowing workshops, held on two Saturdays at the Los Angeles County Arboretum and Botanic Garden in Arcadia and Rancho Cienega Recreation Center in Baldwin Hills during October and November 2014, were open to the public, including individuals who did not have a site. After candidates were counseled about their site's sun exposure, soil quality, water access, and current conditions to assess suitability, one of four custom seed mixes (Coastal, Flatlands, Hillside, and Roadside) was prescribed. The *Wildflowering L.A.* mixes created by the Theodore Payne Foundation correlated with four urban geographies described in Reyner Banham's *Los Angeles: The Architecture of Four Ecologies*, the pioneering 1971 text that guided Haeg's development of the project.

Nearly 300 direct participants planted and tended the fifty sites, playing host to exponentially greater numbers of visitors and passers-by. Participants ranged from master gardeners to curious novices diving into the learning process. Some utilized the project to bring beauty to otherwise empty plots, while parents, teachers, and students nurtured sites at four elementary and middle schools where the project was an educational tool. Front yard gardeners chatted with neighbors, introducing themselves and the native blooms, and in some cases, laminating image guides to disseminate information. Public parks in Watts and Florence-Firestone sowed seed in empty beds, utilizing the hardy Roadside Mix.

During peak bloom and to culminate the year's endeavor, LAND organized an exhibition at The Shed in Northwest Pasadena on April 26–27, 2014. Participants regathered to symbolically place flowers at numbered sites on a large-scale diagrammatic floor map of Los Angeles County freeways, created by Haeg and volunteers. Conversations with key participants, music performances, demonstrations, information offered by the Theodore Payne Foundation, and a display of children's wildflower drawings completed the participatory exhibition.

Through it all, a contribution to the region's native seed bank was restored at each site. The project connected participants on both a micro and macro level — mirroring the structure of the project itself — as bonds were made across socioeconomically diverse parts of the county and simultaneously with admiring next-door neighbors, planting the seed, so to speak, for years to come.

This endeavor of building bonds through community, nature, and art was supported in its entirety by the James Irvine Foundation's Exploring Engagement Fund. LAND would like to take this opportunity to express deep gratitude for the Foundation's support, without which *Wildflowering L.A.* and Fritz Haeg's vision for the project would not have otherwise been realized.

Shamim M. Momin

LAND Director and Curator

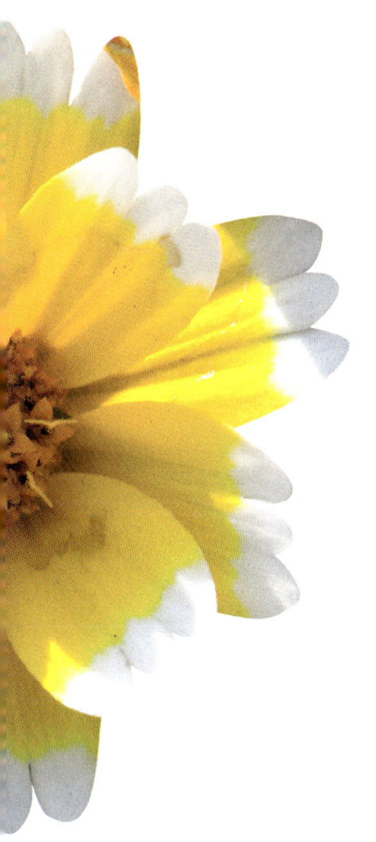

Layia platyglossa (Tidy Tips)

L.A.'s Wild Legacy

Fritz Haeg's inventive *Wildflowering L.A.* invited city dwellers to embrace their own ecological heritage, unite with neighbors and adjoining communities, and revive a dormant local identity. *Wildflowering L.A.* reminded denizens of Los Angeles County how beautiful this urban landscape can be, and how rewarding it is to be actively involved with our land.

Botanical historians can only piece together a vision of the Los Angeles landscape as it existed before the arrival of European settlers. Though it is difficult to say which plants grew in specific neighborhoods, there are clues as to what was here long ago. Journals of late 17th and 18th century Spanish explorer Juan Crespí contained observations of "vastly lush landscapes."[1] Other Spanish explorers described landscapes carpeted with expanses of wildflowers.[2] In addition, pre-1930 herbarium records reflect the abundance of wildflowers in the Los Angeles region. These habitats were quickly affected by European contact. They were first invaded by exotic annual grasses and mustards, and further impacted by grazing practices. By the end of the 19th century, this damage was compounded by urban and early suburban development that included interurban rail lines, housing construction, and the expansion of industry.

When Theodore Payne — father of the native plant movement in California — came to the United States from England in the late 1800s, he was struck by the rapid disappearance of local wildflowers, native landscape, and wildlife. As a trained horticulturist living in a burgeoning Los Angeles, he embarked on a mission to recreate wildflower meadows within the city. One such meadow, installed in 1905 in a vacant lot in Hollywood, gleaned newfound wildflower aficionados.

More than 100 years later, Fritz Haeg was moved to continue Payne's legacy, in modern time and with fresh twists. The *Wildflowering L.A.*

seed sowing initiative was an examination of the places where, to borrow Fritz Haeg's own words, "natural ecology meets urban ecology" and past meets present — a reconsideration of how urban dwellers might cultivate a future that integrates long-term stewardship of the land.

Designed for visual impact, diverse form and color, extended bloom, and habitat value, the custom seed mixes created for *Wildflowering L.A.* by the Theodore Payne Foundation were based on Payne's original formulations developed in the early 1900s. Payne was a progressive nurseryman who collected only small amounts of seed from wild sources and produced second generation seed in an agricultural setting for retail sale. The Theodore Payne Foundation continues to honor this legacy of respecting and protecting our wild lands by offering wildflower seed grown on farms that specialize in native plants or onsite at the Foundation. The four *Wildflowering L.A.* mixes approximated species suited to each of four urban localities: Coastal, Flatlands, Hillside, and Roadside. The Roadside Mix, for example, germinates readily and produces flowers such as California Poppy that thrive in depleted and disturbed soils.

Participants were the heart of the *Wildflowering L.A.* experience. Hardworking, curious, brave, and eager, the *Wildflowering L.A.* participants who planted those seeds were neighborhood ambassadors, enticing passers-by to enjoy the wildflowers, butterflies, and birdsong, as well as to explore the promises and rewards of native plant gardening. Like national and state park signage, the wood signs that marked the *Wildflowering L.A.* meadows signified a crossover between nature as it exists in the wilderness and as part of an urbanized lifestyle, encouraging observers to interact with a project site as they would a natural preserve, to see it as something of value and worth protecting. "*Wildflowering L.A.*-ers" learned the ups and downs of lawn removal, the effect of soil type on seed germination and growth, the challenges of weed management, and the importance of proper watering, especially during a historic drought. Visual aids helped novice gardeners discern a wildflower seedling from a weed and, as the seasons progressed, they learned seeding habits and harvesting tips. The seasonal

1 Crespí, Juan, and Alan K. Brown. *A Description of Distant Roads: Original Journals of the First Expedition into California, 1769–1770.* San Diego: San Diego State University Press, 2001. Print.

2 Minnich, Richard A. *California's Fading Wildflowers: Lost Legacy and Biological Invasions.* Berkeley: University of California Press, 2008. Print.

project timeline mirrored the life cycle of an annual wildflower as it moved from germination to bloom and back to seed again. Throughout the project, updates were posted on the *Wildflowering L.A.* website about issues of concern for these dedicated wildflower meadow stewards and others who were following the project.

Collaborating with Haeg was an honor and a pleasure. We admire how he weaves folks together by common threads — in this case, individuals with an interest in native plants, urban renewal, and resource conservation. He inspired participants to learn new skills and to share and celebrate outcomes, even the unexpected ones. After all, gardening is like that: you follow a plan, do your best to care for the plants, anticipate change, and enjoy what unfolds.

Experiencing the fifty Los Angeles County sites adorned with native color was worthy of celebration! California is a biodiversity hotspot and home to an astonishing number of native plant species, including annual wildflowers whose striking hues and resilient yet ephemeral nature epitomize the beauty and spirit of this region. Just as these plants will regenerate each year, the far-reaching influence of *Wildflowering L.A.* will profoundly echo in the community for years to come. The seed has been planted and awareness cultivated. An indigenous splendor has been reinfused into the local landscape and is thus more likely to endure.

Genevieve Arnold and Lili Singer

Theodore Payne Foundation for Wild Flowers and Native Plants

The Theodore Payne Foundation would like to thank LAND (Los Angeles Nomadic Division) as the organizational body presenting Wildflowering L.A. *They curated the project, managed the details, gathered support, and, at every stage, deftly tended to this work from inception to completion.*

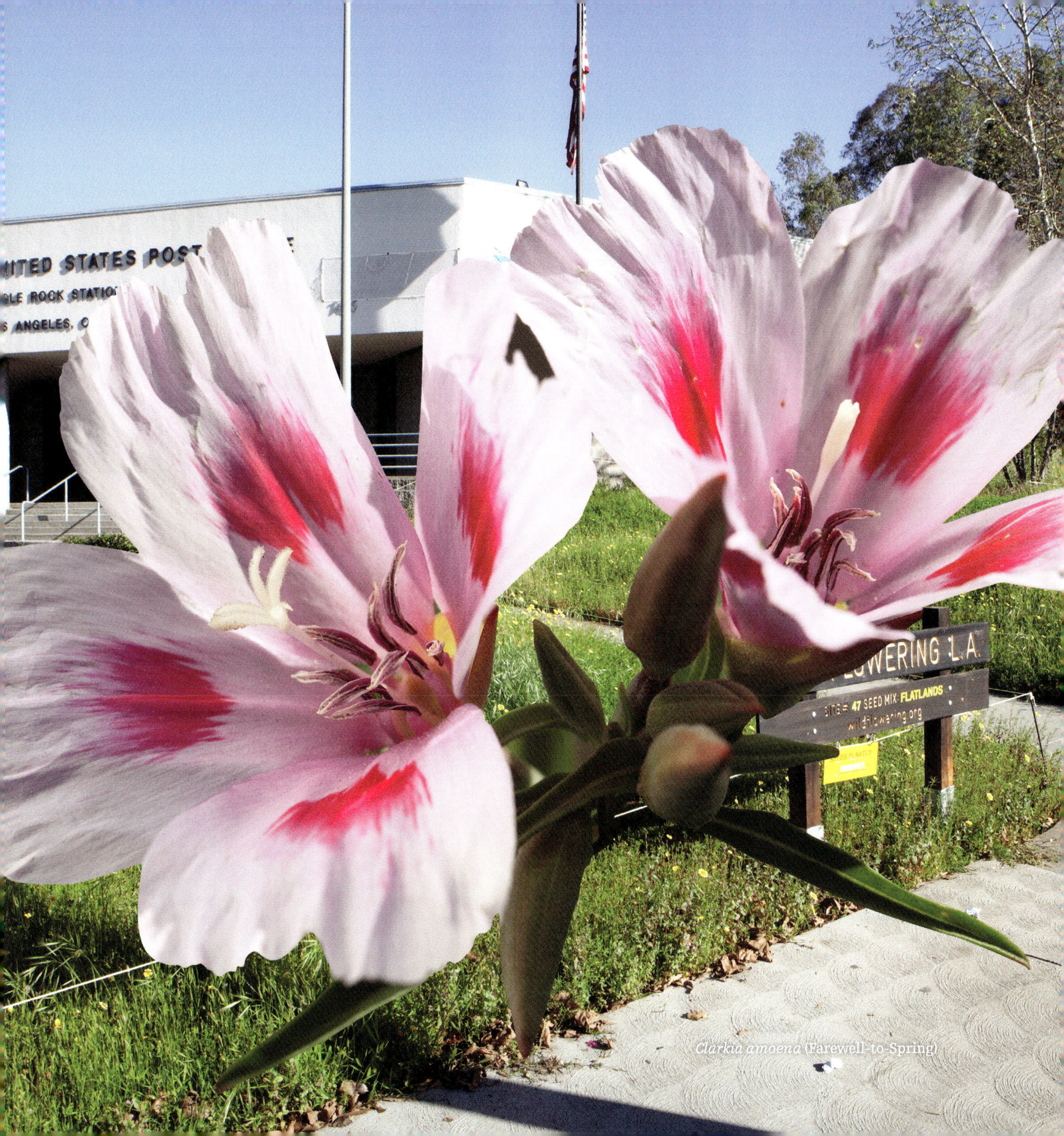

Clarkia amoena (Farewell-to-Spring)

WILDFLOWERING L.A. OPEN CALL FOR SITES

OCTOBER 2013

LAND (Los Angeles Nomadic Division) is placing an open call throughout Los Angeles County for apartment complexes, businesses, child care centers, churches, community centers, hospitals, hotels, offices buildings, schools, senior centers, shopping malls, stores, vacant lots, and more with publicly visible open land ready for some seasonal, colorful, wild, beautiful reconsideration.

Wildflowering L.A. brings a wild and beautiful seasonal native landscape to fifty sites selected from an open call based on public visibility and distribution across the county. Owners of selected sites are given free native wildflower seed mixes at workshops in partnership with the Theodore Payne Foundation. Soil preparation, seeding, and wildflower tending are demonstrated, and one of four custom wildflower seed mixes is prescribed — Coastal, Flatlands, Hillside, and Roadside — inspired by Reyner Banham's 1971 book, *Los Angeles: The Architecture of Four Ecologies*. Each of the participating sites is officially identified with a prominent carved wood sign.

INTERESTED IN PARTICIPATING?

+ You should have ownership of (or permission from the owner to plant) an open plot of land that is sunny and completely visible from a public street, with easy access to water for establishing the seedlings.

+ Seeds are provided for areas from 500 to 2,000 square feet.

+ A 3' x 5' wood sign is installed on each site by the project team after the seeds are planted by the owners in November.

+ Each site will be identified on a published map, and photographed before and after the seeds have been sown for the spring culminating exhibition.

+ Please email a photo of the site taken from the street or public viewing spot and the complete address for consideration.

PUBLIC WORKSHOPS:

Sunday, October 27, 2013, 11am – 5pm
Los Angeles County Arboretum and
Botanic Garden
301 North Baldwin Avenue
Arcadia, CA 91007

Saturday, November 2, 2013, 11am – 5pm
Rancho Cienega Recreation Center
5001 Rodeo Road
Los Angeles, CA 90016

In October 2013, this open call was distributed across Los Angeles County through workshops at farmers markets and garden events, as well as through specialized permaculture and time banking listservs, neighborhood bulletins, newspaper articles, word of mouth, and with the help of civic groups such as the Los Angeles County Arts Commission.

Eschscholzia californica (California Poppy)

COASTAL SEED MIX

+ *Camissoniopsis cheiranthifolia* (Beach Suncups)
+ *Eschscholzia californica* var. *maritima* (California Coastal Poppy)
+ *Gilia capitata* (Globe Gilia)
+ *Leptosiphon grandiflorus* (Large Flower Linanthus)
+ *Lupinus bicolor* (Miniature Lupine)
+ *Lupinus succulentus* (Arroyo Lupine)

FLATLANDS SEED MIX

+ *Achillea millefolium* (White Yarrow)
+ *Clarkia purpurea* (Winecup Clarkia)
+ *Clarkia unguiculata* (Elegant Clarkia)
+ *Eschscholzia californica* (California Poppy)
+ *Gilia tricolor* (Bird's-Eye Gilia)
+ *Layia platyglossa* (Tidy Tips)
+ *Lupinus truncatus* (Collared Annual Lupine)
+ *Stipa pulchra* (Purple Needlegrass)

HILLSIDE SEED MIX

+ *Clarkia amoena* (Farewell-to-Spring)
+ *Clarkia unguiculata* (Elegant Clarkia)
+ *Eschscholzia californica* (California Poppy)
+ *Gilia capitata* (Globe Gilia)
+ *Layia platyglossa* (Tidy Tips)
+ *Linum lewisii* (Blue Flax)
+ *Lupinus succulentus* (Arroyo Lupine)
+ *Mentzelia lindleyi* (Blazing Star)
+ *Lasthenia californica* (Goldfields)
+ *Phacelia minor* (California Bluebell)
+ *Phacelia tanacetifolia* (Lacy Phacelia)

ROADSIDE SEED MIX

+ *Amsinckia menziesii* (Fiddleneck)
+ *Clarkia unguiculata* (Elegant Clarkia)
+ *Eschscholzia californica* (California Poppy)
+ *Gilia capitata* (Globe Gilia)
+ *Gilia tricolor* (Bird's-Eye Gilia)
+ *Layia platyglossa* (Tidy Tips)
+ *Lupinus succulentus* (Arroyo Lupine)
+ *Phacelia tanacetifolia* (Lacy Phacelia)

The seed mixes prescribed to each of the fifty *Wildflowering L.A.* sites were customized by the experts of the Theodore Payne Foundation based on climate and soil type. Create your own mix inspired by the project using the seed varieties appropriate to your ecology.

Tips for making your garden thrive! Participants in *Wildflowering L.A.* received consultations and seasonal instructions on establishing and maintaining their native California wildflower gardens from Genevieve Arnold, Seed Program Manager, and Lili Singer, Director of Special Projects and Adult Education, at the Theodore Payne Foundation.

FALL: Site Prep and Sowing

PREPARING THE SITE

Remove existing weeds or grass without tilling any deeper than 3 to 4 inches; deeper tilling beyond 3 to 4 inches will most likely unearth deeply embedded, dormant weed seeds and encourage their germination, thus increasing weed growth! It is best to leave these deeply buried seeds undisturbed in a dormant state beneath the soil. Plant a small sample of the seed in pots, so that you can learn to identify which seedlings are the desired wildflowers and which are weeds to be removed as your wildflower garden progresses.

SOWING THE SEED

METHOD I: HORTICULTURAL SAND

Combine 1 part seed to 3 parts horticultural sand ("sharp sand" made of washed, lime-free quartzite). Scatter the mixture evenly. This method is effective because the sand helps protect the seed from hungry birds. A single layer of pea gravel can also guard seed from birds waiting in the wings. If desired, bird netting can be attached to stakes and stretched across the top and around sides of the area.

METHOD II: SCATTER & COVER

Scatter seed evenly and cover with a bit of soil (either your own garden soil or a light potting soil). The seed should not be sown deeper than 1/8" beneath the soil surface. Apply just enough soil to cover; do not bury the seed.

METHOD III: SCATTER & RAKE

Scatter seed and then gently rake with a standard leaf rake so that seed doesn't get pushed down too deeply under the soil surface. Horticultural sand or a light potting soil may be used to cover the seed, but keep in mind that the seed should be sown just below (approximately 1/8") the soil surface.

TIPS FOR SPECIAL SITUATIONS

Clay Soil: Loosen the top couple of inches and smooth over. After seed is scattered, use the backside of a leaf rake to gently beat the seed into the soil surface, taking care not to overdo it and injure the seed. This will push the seed down just slightly into the soil crevices. Raking hard clay soil using the front of the rake may be ineffective or create a clumping effect, wherein the seed is unable to germinate because it is buried under chunks of soil.

Slopes: It can be helpful to wet down the area thoroughly before sowing to help seeds stick; after the seeds are sown, be sure to water them in immediately and thoroughly. To prevent seeds from washing down the slope with the rains, it can be helpful to lightly walk on the soil surface to secure the seeds into the soil, as long as this action can be performed gently, without slippage. Placing a flat board over sown areas and then walking on it will probably cause less soil disturbance than footsteps alone!

Pets and foot traffic: If the area is frequented by active pets or foot traffic, cordon or block it off after planting while the wildflowers are establishing.

WATERING AND CARE

"Water in" your seed immediately after sowing. Use an oscillating hose nozzle, a shower or fan spray hose attachment, or a sprinkler with a soft, even spray from your irrigation system. Water very thoroughly but gently, passing back and forth over the area so that seed stays firmly in place, and avoid creating pooling and flooding effects.

Several initial thorough watering sessions are very important, as they help secure the seed in the soil and ensure that the seed has firm seed-to-soil contact. The seed should not be buried deeply into the soil, nor should it be sitting loose and unprotected on the soil surface.

It is recommended to sow the seed in advance of fall rains (typically in October or November) and water manually, so that by the time storms do come more frequently, the seed is set securely in the soil and will not be washed away.

Keep the soil consistently moist until a few inches of growth are visible, and then water as needed when the top couple of inches of soil are dry. Avoid watterlogging. Even if intermittent rainstorms occur, seedlings must be watered between rain events. Do not allow ungerminated seeds or small, delicate seedlings to dry out. They need that constant moisture to become well established.

Once your wildflowers are blooming, occasional deep watering will extend the duration of the flowering period.

WINTER: Weeding and Watering

ON WEEDING

It is exciting to see wildflower seedlings emerge and grow. However, it can be disconcerting to observe weeds coming up right beside them. This common problem in sowing wildflower meadows can be addressed with a few hours dedicated to weeding on a regular basis throughout the growing season.

As you weed, don't worry too much about trampling or damaging existing wildflower seedlings when entering your sow site. Each mature wildflower plant will occupy about ½ to 1 square foot of space, so some loss will not affect the overall appearance of your meadow.

ESTABLISH A WEEDING AREA

Stones: Place paver stones at a few locations within the site. Once the plants have matured, they will visually block the staggered paths and the pavers either won't show or will still look attractive. In addition, these spots can serve as vantage points from which to photograph flowers, insects, and birds come spring!

Pathways: Create a few narrow pathways (perhaps three or so, depending upon the size of the area) and use them to enter the site for weeding. Establishing these thoroughfares can be as easy as choosing where you will walk and sit, akin to a deer selecting its favorite point of access through a meadow and walking the path repeatedly. Plants in your pathways may be completely removed, or just walked on and not removed. This way, tough seedlings that do survive will still have a chance to develop.

WEED REMOVAL TIPS

Identify the weed: The weeding method will depend on the nature of the targeted weed, which will most likely fall into one of four categories: exotic annual weed, exotic annual bunch grass, exotic perennial weed, or exotic perennial lawn grass. Commonly found exotic, non-native annual weeds in Southern California include Cheeseweed and Australian Brass Buttons. Exotic, non-native perennial weeds and lawn grasses include *Oxalis stricta* (Wood Sorrel), *Oxalis pes-caprae* (Bermuda Buttercup), and Bermuda grass.

Exotic annual weeds and bunch grasses: These may be pulled out from the base at ground level. While this method may displace some desired seedlings, that is probably just fine depending on the number of native wildflower seedlings within the plot. The volume of seeds prescribed to each site's square footage accounts for some attrition or loss of seedlings. Alternately, with narrow snips or clippers, go in at the base of the weed just below the soil surface and cut. The roots will remain underground but will desiccate and die once detached from the top growth.

Exotic perennial weeds and lawn grasses: If the perennial weeds have deep roots, they must be removed entirely — roots and all — to prevent them from returning. A trowel or "dandelion digger" that gets under the main plant to help you pull is an excellent tool for the job. Deep-rooted rhizomatous grasses, such as Bermuda, are not controlled by cuts just below the surface. In fact, cutting the rhizomes will actually stimulate growth. Sprigs and clumps of Bermuda grass must be completely removed from the base of the outgrowth with as many roots as possible — but dig no deeper than four inches to avoid bringing up weed seeds and disturbing surrounding plants.

Weed disposal: Dispose of weeds in your regular household trashcan, rather than in the green waste bin. This way, weeds and their seed are treated as refuse and do not have the opportunity to regenerate in a wider sphere. If weeds go into the green waste bin or compost, the mulch created will harbor the weed seeds and further propagate the very plants we are trying to eradicate.

ON WATERING

California experienced its driest year on record in 2013–2014. Compounding scant rainfall with persistent, drying Santa Ana winds in Los Angeles County, our landscapes became stressed. We can learn about what our urban gardens will do by looking to nature; if our wild areas are showing signs of drought stress, our cultivated gardens will certainly follow suit.

Now that your wildflower seedlings have reached a couple of inches in height, you may have cut back on the vigorous watering schedule used to germinate and establish the seeds. You may notice that, while your seedlings are not wilting, they also aren't showing signs of growth and are maintaining a low height.

In dry circumstances, we recommend a deep watering of the site every seven to ten days, especially through warm and windy spells. Watch the seedlings closely; if you see signs of wilting or discoloration, then apply deeper and more frequent watering until they stabilize.

If dry weather continues, your wildflower meadows will boast a much showier and longer bloom if they continue to receive a periodic watering. Regular irrigation will also increase the chances of a healthy seed set, ensuring that the wildflowers come back in good number next year.

The response of seedlings at each site will vary. Watch your meadow and get to know how the seedlings are responding to a special weather period.

In the process, you'll be brought closer to your garden and to the natural world as it responds to our unique climate.

Keep in mind that even if you are watering every 10 days or so, you're still using much less water than a thirsty exotic lawn would require to stay green during a drought!

Sowing seed always involves some unpredictable variables respective to each unique site, and you will learn as you go. A fully flush meadow may not occur in the first year of sowing. You can prepare your soil again over the summer and re-sow next fall, with the advantage of the knowledge gained in this initial year of gardening experience. The important thing is that you have taken the first step to establishing a native landscape. Take a moment to pat yourself on the back for your hard work, patience, and meaningful contribution to our precious ecosystem here in Los Angeles!

SPRING: Seed Harvest After the Bloom

In Los Angeles County, we find ourselves in a slightly confusing stage of weather where we ask the question "Is it spring or summer?" May feels like a transitional month between the two seasons. Some days can reach upwards of 90°F, while other days are at a pleasant 75°F.

The annual wildflowers in your meadow are feeling the same way. Some early blooming species took a cue from the summer-like heat and have already gone to seed (Tidy Tips and Lupines, for example) or are starting to brown up, while others are still in spring bloom (including Elegant Clarkia, Farewell-to-Spring, some California Poppy, and Globe Gilia). As your meadow transitions with the season, you may wonder what to do next in terms of maintenance.

If you leave the spent flower heads in place for a while, the birds will consume some of the seed (always fun to observe) and some of the seed will go into the soil bank where it will rest until it receives its germination cues next fall. Should you wish to help the seed scattering process along a bit, you can shake the spent flowers directly over your ground.

Some gardeners enjoy harvesting the seed and storing it for sowing in the fall, or sharing with friends and neighbors who have admired the showy wildflower display.

Seed is ripe when the flower head is tan or brown and slightly crunchy without being fried to a crisp. Place spent flower stalks upside down in a paper bag so the seed can dehisce on its own. Place the bag in a cool, aerated, and dry area up off the ground for two weeks. During the drying and dehiscing period, seed will drop to the bottom of the bag. That seed can then be labeled, placed in a jar, and stashed in a cool, dark, dry closet or cupboard until next fall.

Perhaps you are intending to clear and prepare your ground over the summer in preparation for planting native perennials in the fall. Should you wish to remove the spent plants entirely after leaving them for the birds to enjoy, they do pull up easily and can be added to compost or green bins; this way, any seed remaining within the plant material has an increased chance of regenerating. The removal of dry plant material might be the most appropriate option for sites in fire-sensitive areas. This process can be done gradually so that the flowers in bloom remain and the dried matter is removed.

This phase of the native wildflower meadow is an especially intriguing one. As bright blooms give way to the muted tones of next year's seed bank, we are reminded that each phase of the cycle provides habitat essential to the survival of local animal and insect species and is beautiful in its own way.

SEED HARVEST INSTRUCTIONS

GENERAL TIPS

+ Use durable, secure cloth or paper bags (not plastic) to capture seed. Paper and cloth absorb moisture, which prevents molding.
+ Harvest when plant material is completely dry; don't harvest wet or damp fruit or seed.
+ Dried wildflower stalks may be clipped off at the base, which serves the dual purpose of removing spent material for the season.

+ Place stalks upside-down in the bag; many species will dehisce (discharge seed) on their own.
+ Alternatively, the bag may be held beneath the inflorescence (flower head) and you may use your hands to gently separate the seed head. The bag will capture the crumbled plant material.

AFTER THE HARVEST

+ Place the bag containing plant material to dry for approximately two weeks in a cool, dry area protected from rodents.
+ Airflow is important; if seed sits for long periods of time in stifling and/or humid conditions, it will likely not maintain good viability.
+ After the drying period, place the seed in a clean jar and store in the back of a cool, dry cupboard until next fall's sowing season.

SUMMER: Solarization

Late June brings an official shift of season, as the sun is at its highest point of the year on the Summer Solstice. Your meadows may still be dotted with a few bright orange California Poppy, blazing pink Farewell-to-Spring, or powder-purple Globe Gilia; others may have completely browned and gone to seed.

As we launch into summer, the question for many is: "What's next?" This hiatus in the growing cycle is the perfect opportunity to prepare for fall planting and sowing. The preparation has two parts: Study and Action.

PART ONE: STUDY

How about relaxing in a favorite chair on a shady porch with a book on native plants? *California Native Plants for the Garden* by Carol Bornstein, David Fross, and Bart O'Brien is a comprehensive, full color, and easy-to-navigate option. Consider the plants that appeal to you, and which will do well with your climate, sun exposure, and soil type. Want birds and butterflies? Color and fragrance? Summer shade? Drought tolerance? A truly amazing palette of native plants and wildflowers awaits your discovery. Theodore Payne Foundation's online Native Plant Database also has particulars on more than 1,000 California native plants. Or, attend a California Native Plant Horticulture Class in the Theodore Payne Foundation's Education Center to learn the basics on gardening with California flora: why native plant communities are valuable, planting techniques, establishment, irrigation, pruning, and ongoing maintenance.

PART TWO: ACTION

Over the course of eight months, many sites dealt with the emergence of weeds. The hottest months of the year can be utilized to address this issue by preparing the ground for fall planting and sowing. One way to diminish next year's weed crop is to solarize areas in full sun come July or August. This is a method of applying plastic sheeting in order to "heat-kill" weed seeds in the soil bank.

Only during the hottest, high summer months when days are long and temperatures soar can gardeners perform soil solarization — a non-chemical control for soil borne pests, including those dreaded weed seeds. Soil solarization works best in areas with full sun (no shade) and is most effective inland, where summer days are consistently hot and fog-free.

When done right, an enormous number of weed seeds are killed, meaning your next wildflower meadow (or new native garden, if you're converting to long-lived perennial plants) will be more beautiful and easier to maintain. Less weeding means more time to watch the bees, butterflies, and other beneficial insects that love to visit native flowers!

SOLARIZING BASICS

+ Clear the area of all plant material and any sharp objects such as rocks.
+ Wet the soil thoroughly to a depth of 6".
+ Dig a 6" deep trench around the perimeter of the area.
+ Lay clear (not black) 1.5–4 mil plastic on the soil surface, stretching it tightly to the edges and down into the trenches.
+ Fill the trenches with soil to secure the plastic very tightly — as tightly as possible so that no air gets in (air cools down the process and defeats the purpose).
+ Leave the plastic in place for 4–6 weeks.

For solarizing to work, you should see condensation (water droplets) under the plastic but no plant growth. Ideally, the soil will heat up to 140°F, a temperature that few weed seeds can survive!

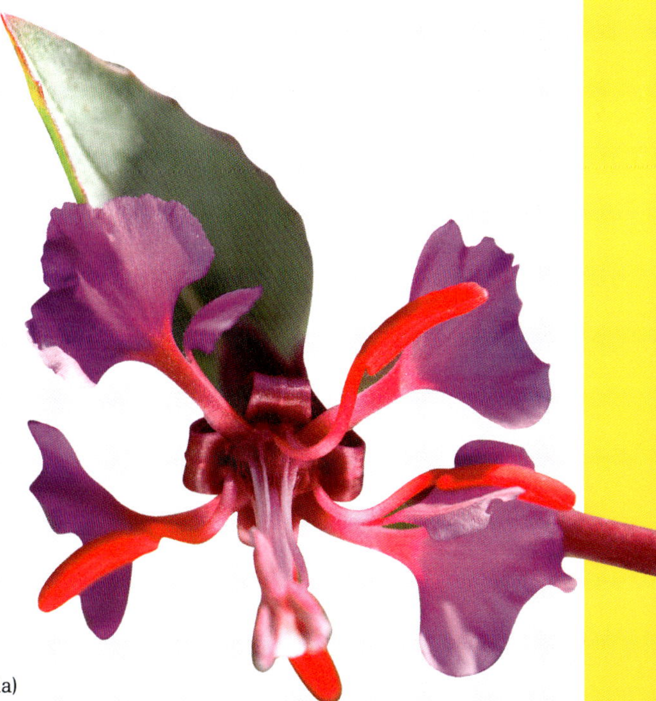

Clarkia unguiculata (Elegant Clarkia)

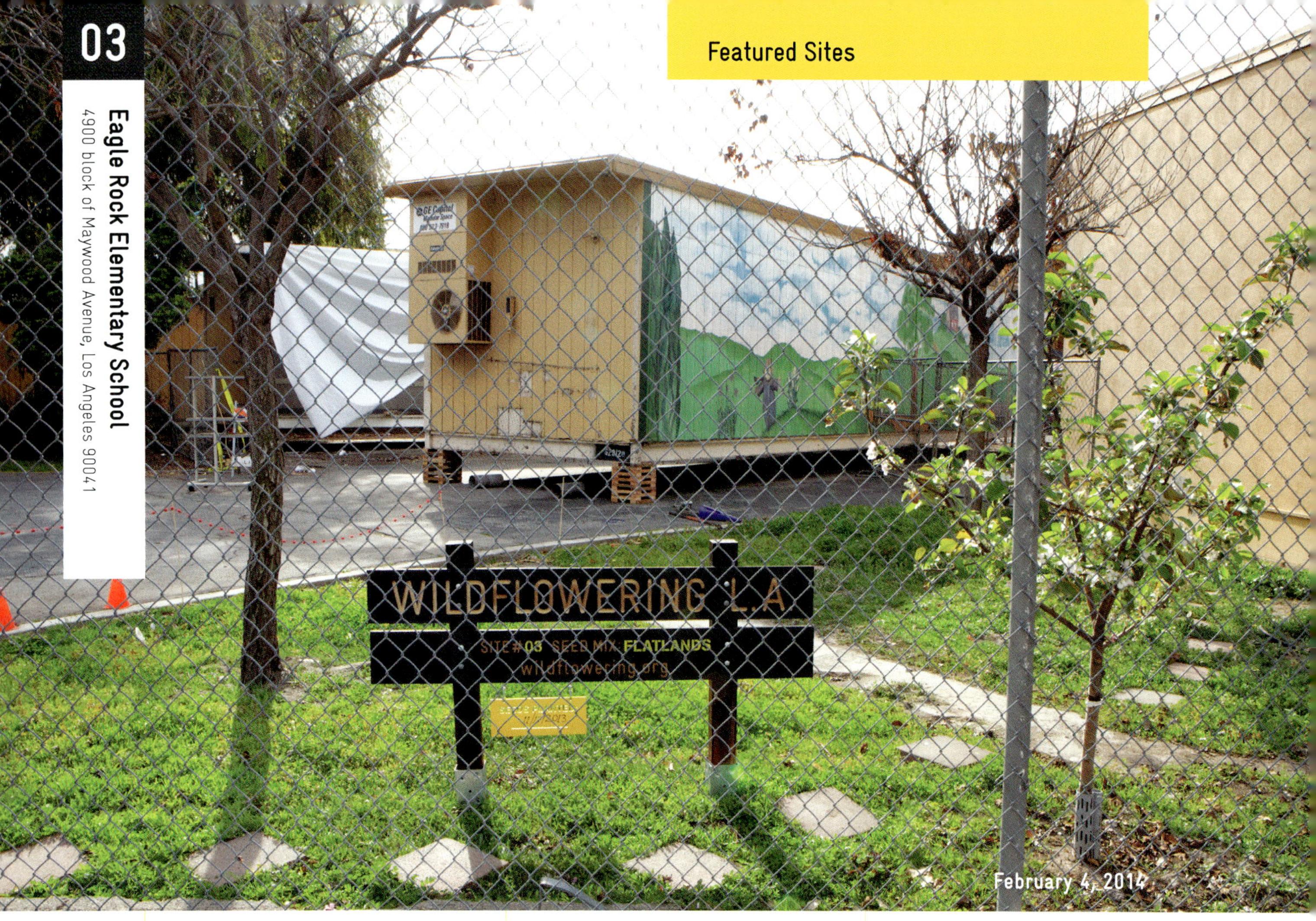

Eagle Rock Elementary School
4900 block of Maywood Avenue, Los Angeles 90041

MAR 8 There was near tragedy and a wonderful hero in the story of our wildflower meadow. After winter break, and fortunately during recess when students were playing nearby, a substitute district gardener took it upon himself to start keeping the "grass" (also known as our budding wildflowers) under control. Fifteen impassioned 5th graders who had sowed, cared for, and watered the meadow besieged the gardener. One student, angered by this transgression, actually placed himself in the line of the weed-wacker and refused to move until the gardener left the site. An informational sign designating the area as a "No Mow Zone" was created in response by students in Ms. Reeves' 5th grade class so that everyone could understand the importance of the meadow.

JUN 18 Being part of *Wildflowering L.A.* was such an honor. I know our community felt very proud. All our special deliveries that came through that gate received special instructions on how precious that area was, and how they had better not carelessly back up over it! We will keep the site going as natives.

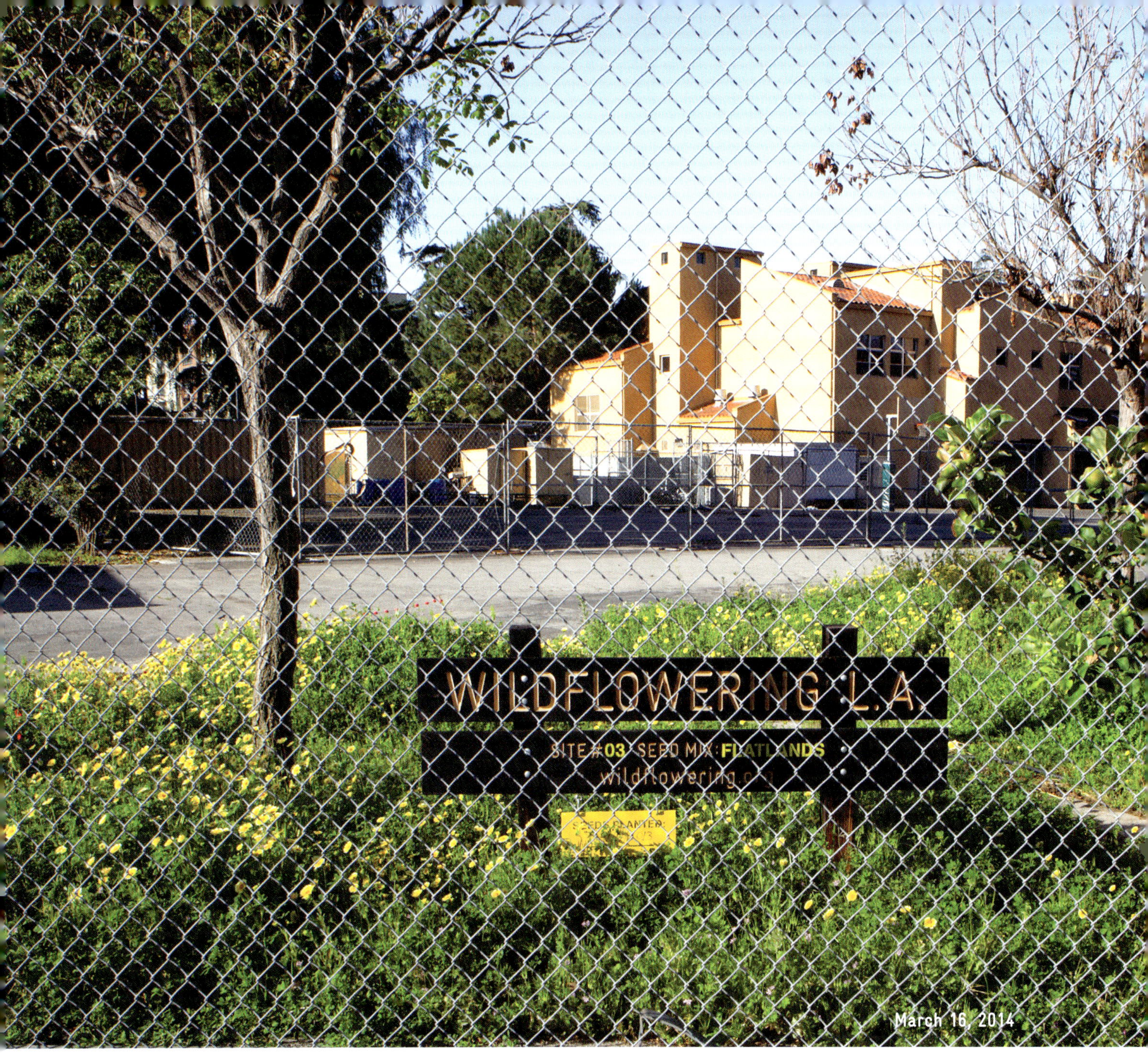

Planted by students, parents, and teachers of Eagle Rock Elementary School.

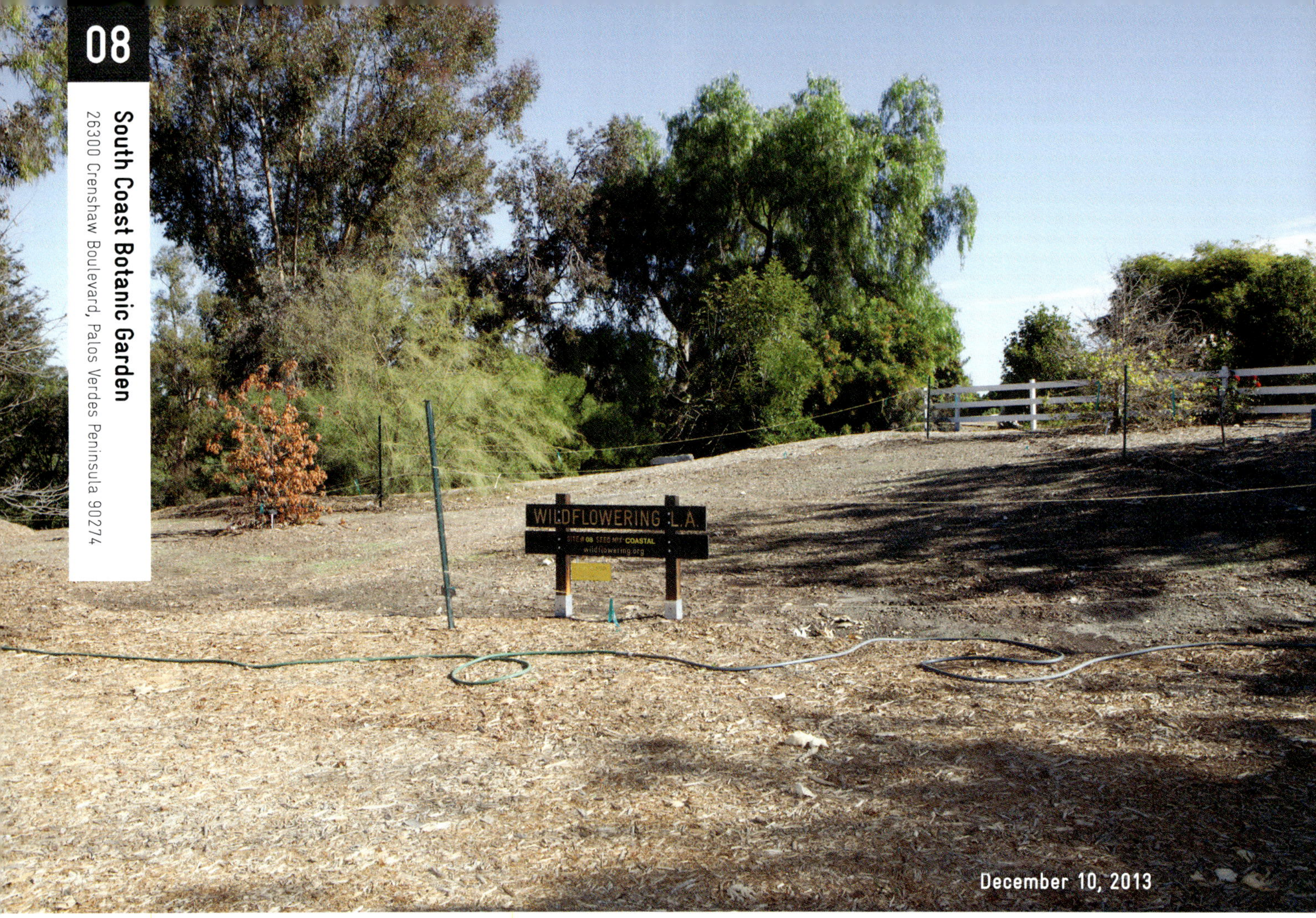

FEB 25 With all of the new seedlings coming in, peak bloom of our Coastal Mix will be the end of March. It might actually be worth deadheading the early Lupine to encourage more blooming.

MAY 15 Some flowers are still blooming!

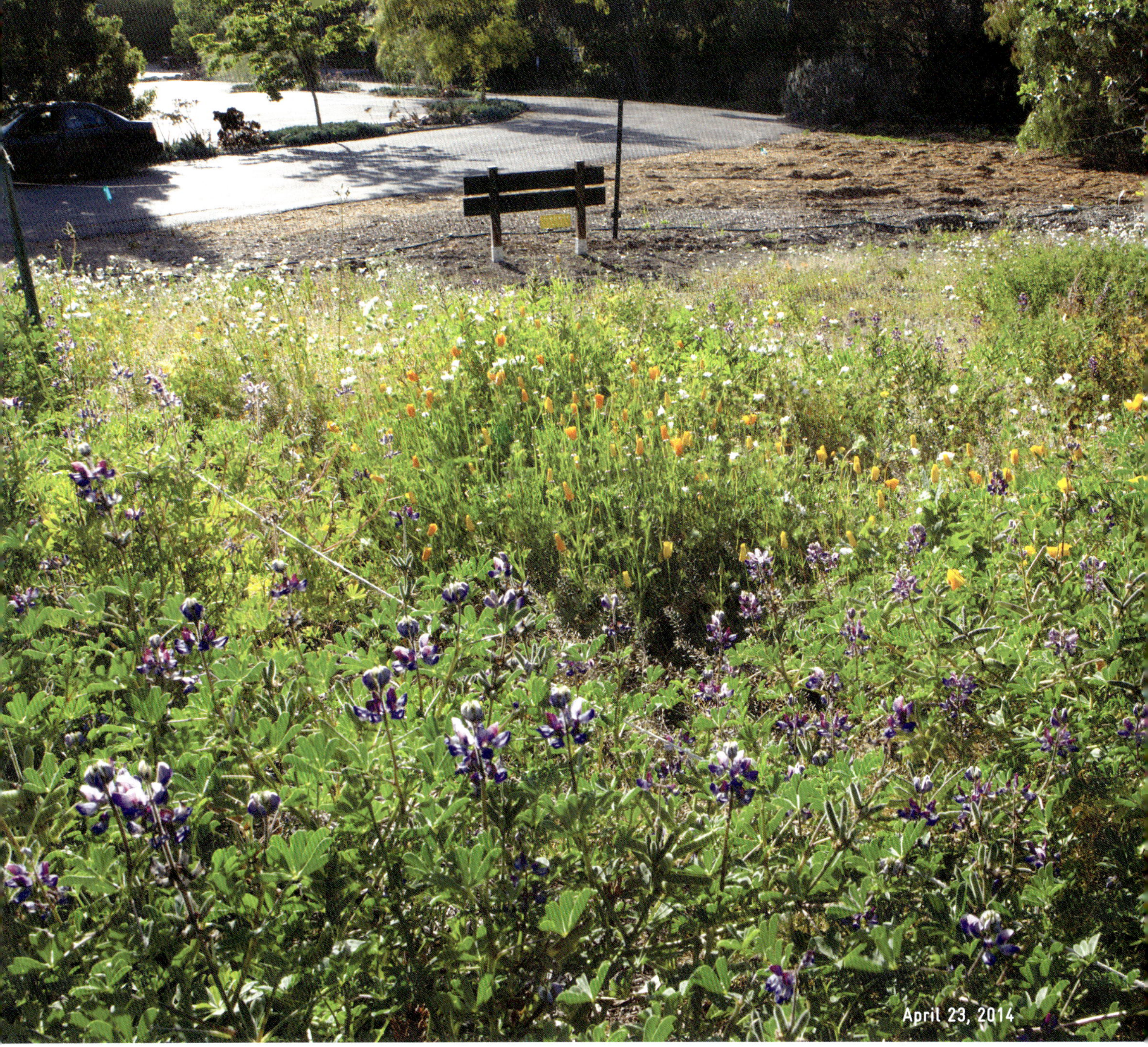
April 23, 2014

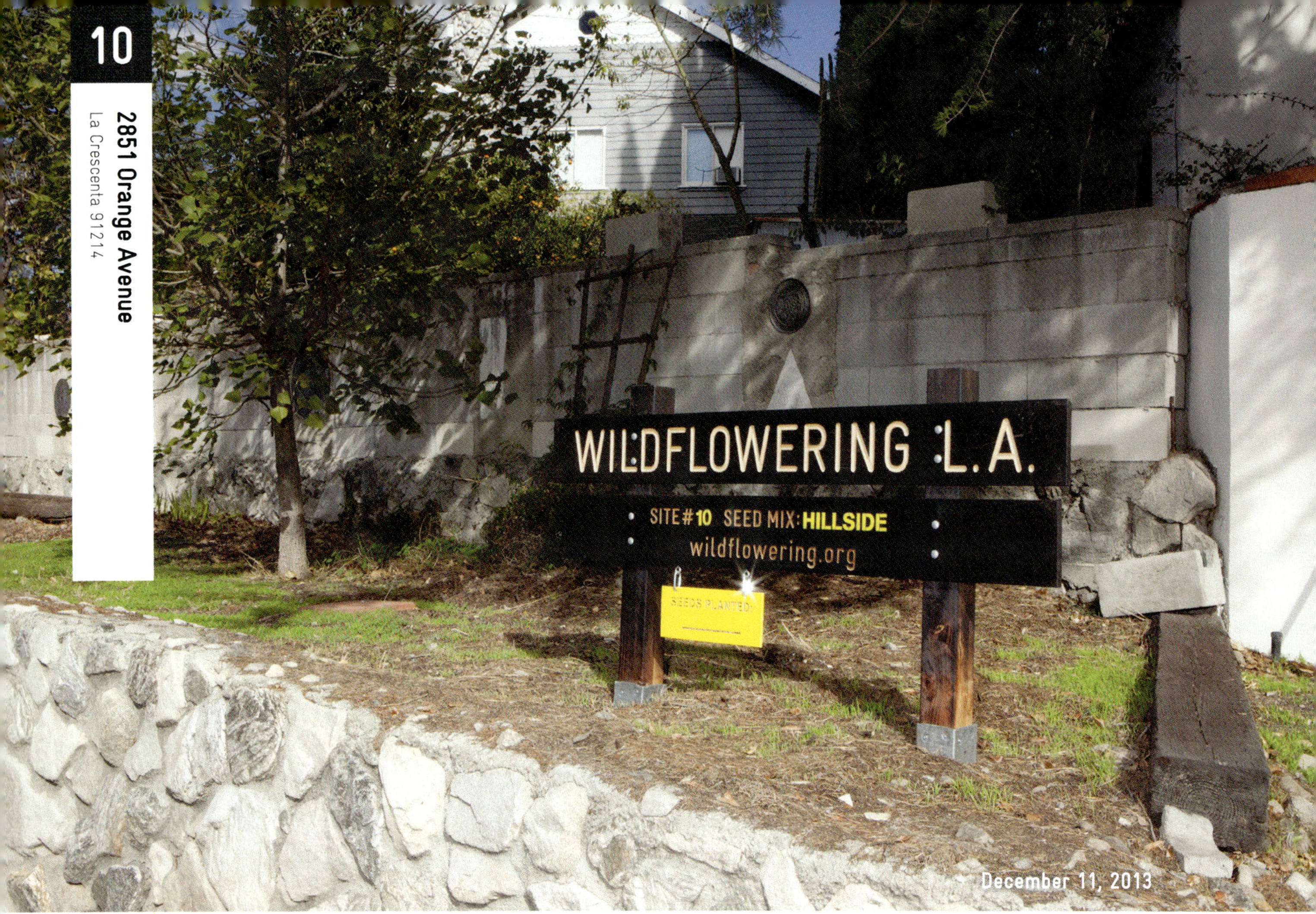

MAR 6 In bloom now and changing every week...I think the peak week might be the first or second week of April.

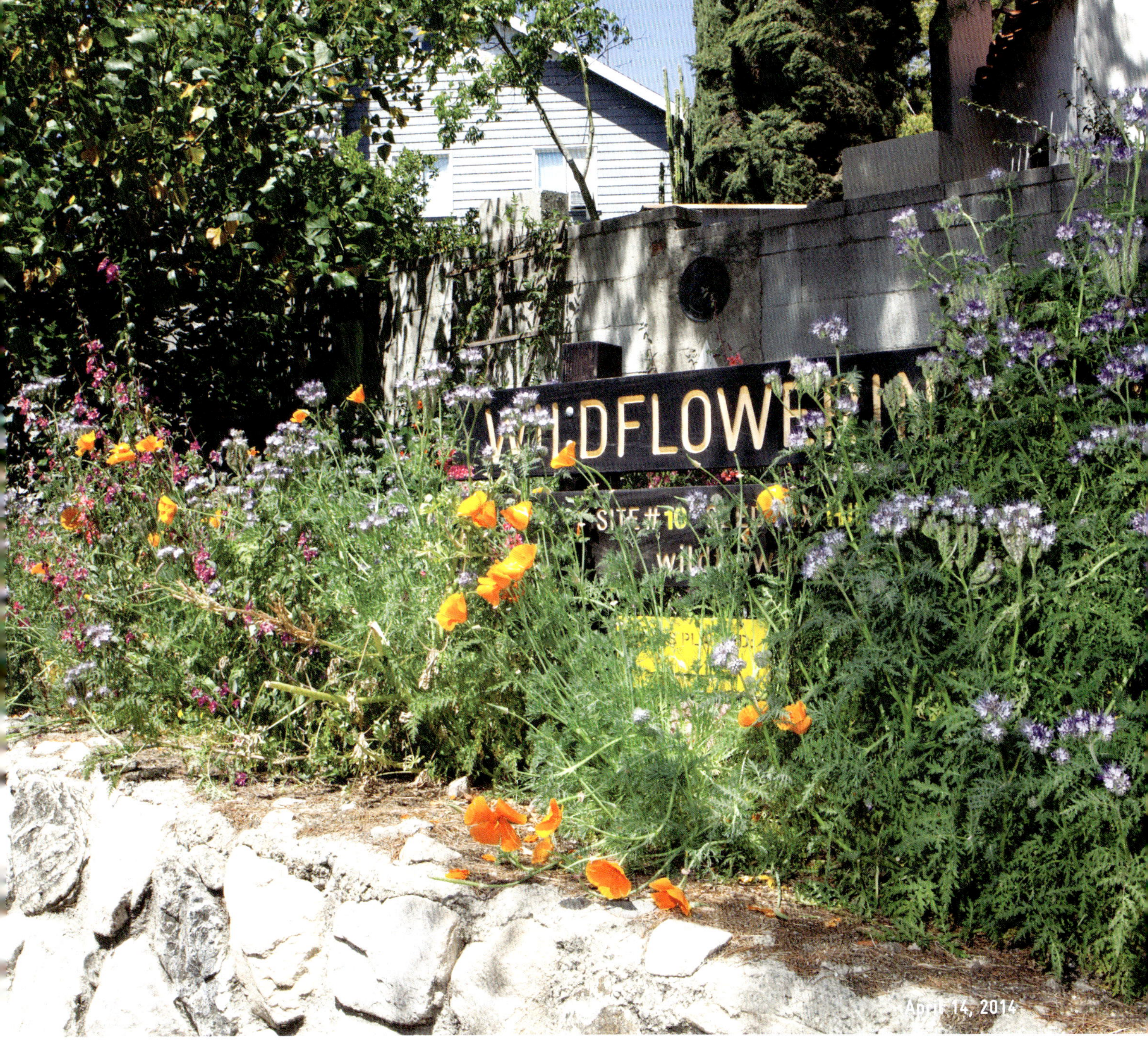
WiLDFLOWER IN
SITE #10
wild
April 14, 2014

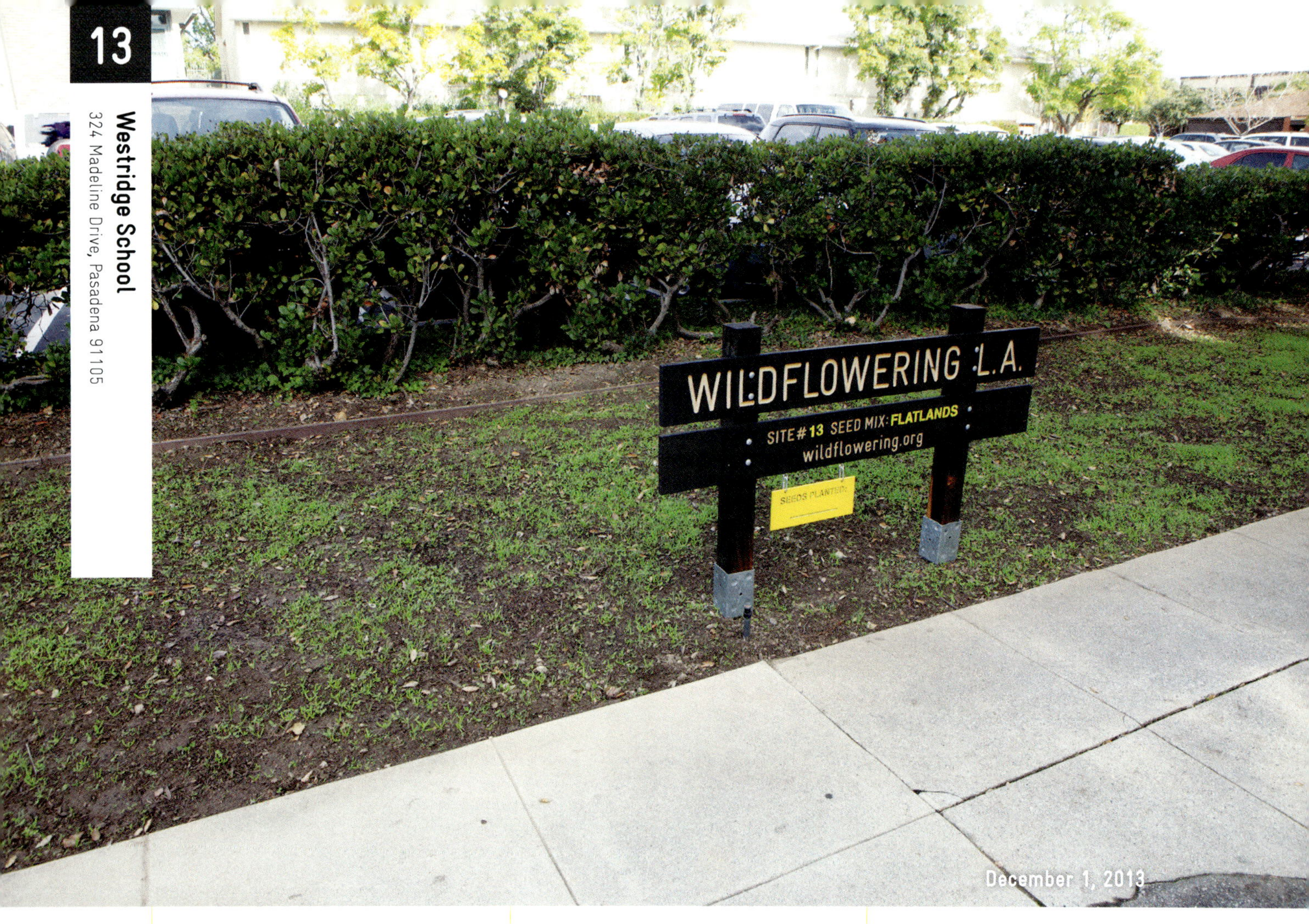

MAR 14 First Lupine and first Elegant Clarkia and first Bird's-Eye Gilia! I think this garden is at least three to four weeks away from a spectacular bloom. The *Achillea* (White Yarrow) has just reached "baby" size and no sign of the *Stipa* (Purple Needlegrass). This garden is shaded a good deal of the day by a large oak. For that reason, the east end of the patch is weeks behind the west end, which is just starting to show color other than the early-blooming yellow and white *Layia* (Tidy Tips). I expect that this garden will be excellent, but will come in much later than the others.

JUN 20 I have gotten nothing but compliments about the wildflower display. We have harvested a great deal of seed and should be able to continue the lovely tradition in the future. We would probably just like to add new seed varieties to the palette for more diversity and a longer blooming season.

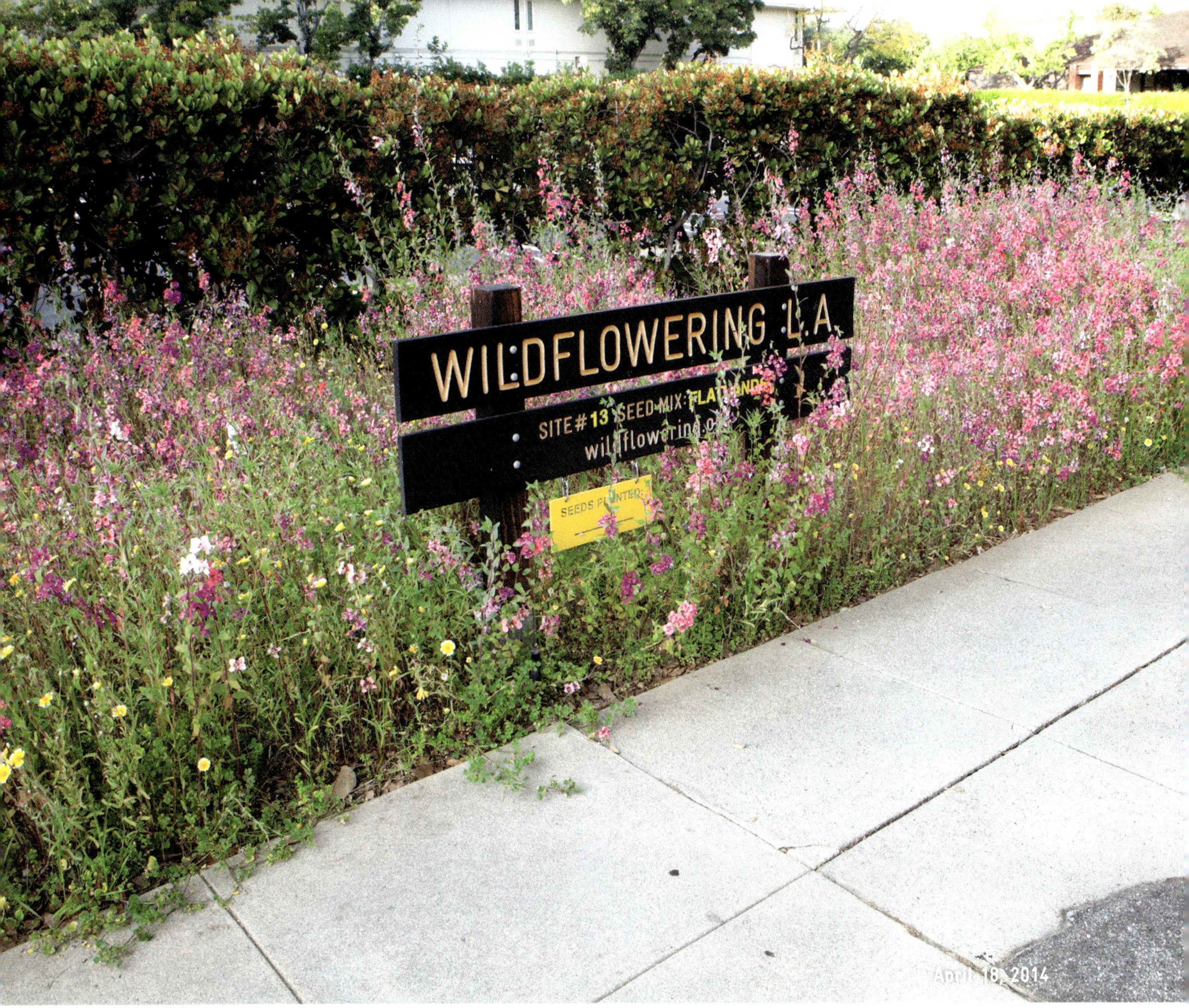

Planted by 7th grade students in Westridge's Community Action Project in collaboration with the
Los Angeles County Arboretum and Botanic Garden.

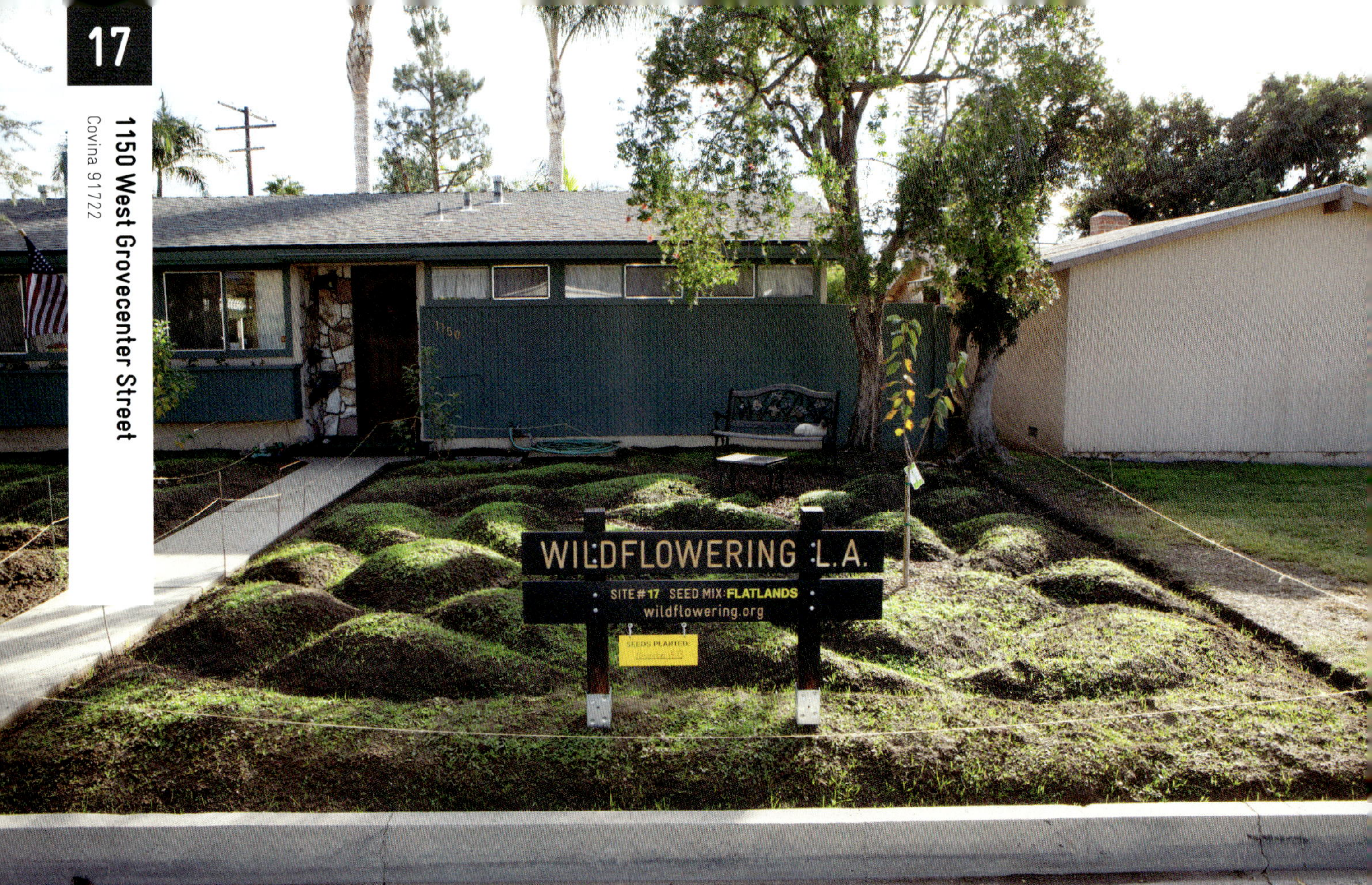

MAR 10 It looks truly beautiful, and only has some spots where animals trampled on it. My front yard is on the north side of the house and I have some trees in it as well. As the sun moves, the flowering plants open and bloom accordingly. The peak, I think, is happening in the next week to the next month.

MAY 20 Our front yard is pretty much dried up. We still have some California Poppy blooming but the White Yarrow never appeared except for one single flower, and my Purple Needlegrass is also gone for some reason. The drought was just too much for my plants out here in the San Gabriel Valley. Heat out here was above 90°F and 100°F. Brutal!

JUN 23 Our *Wildflowering L.A.* site is far from over. Our plan is to redesign our yard this fall to include not just the native wildflowers, but more native perennials that attract bees and butterflies. We are going to register our site this fall as a Monarch Butterfly Waystation. Our site will continue to grow towards sustainability and we hope to create a model for our neighborhood, our city, and

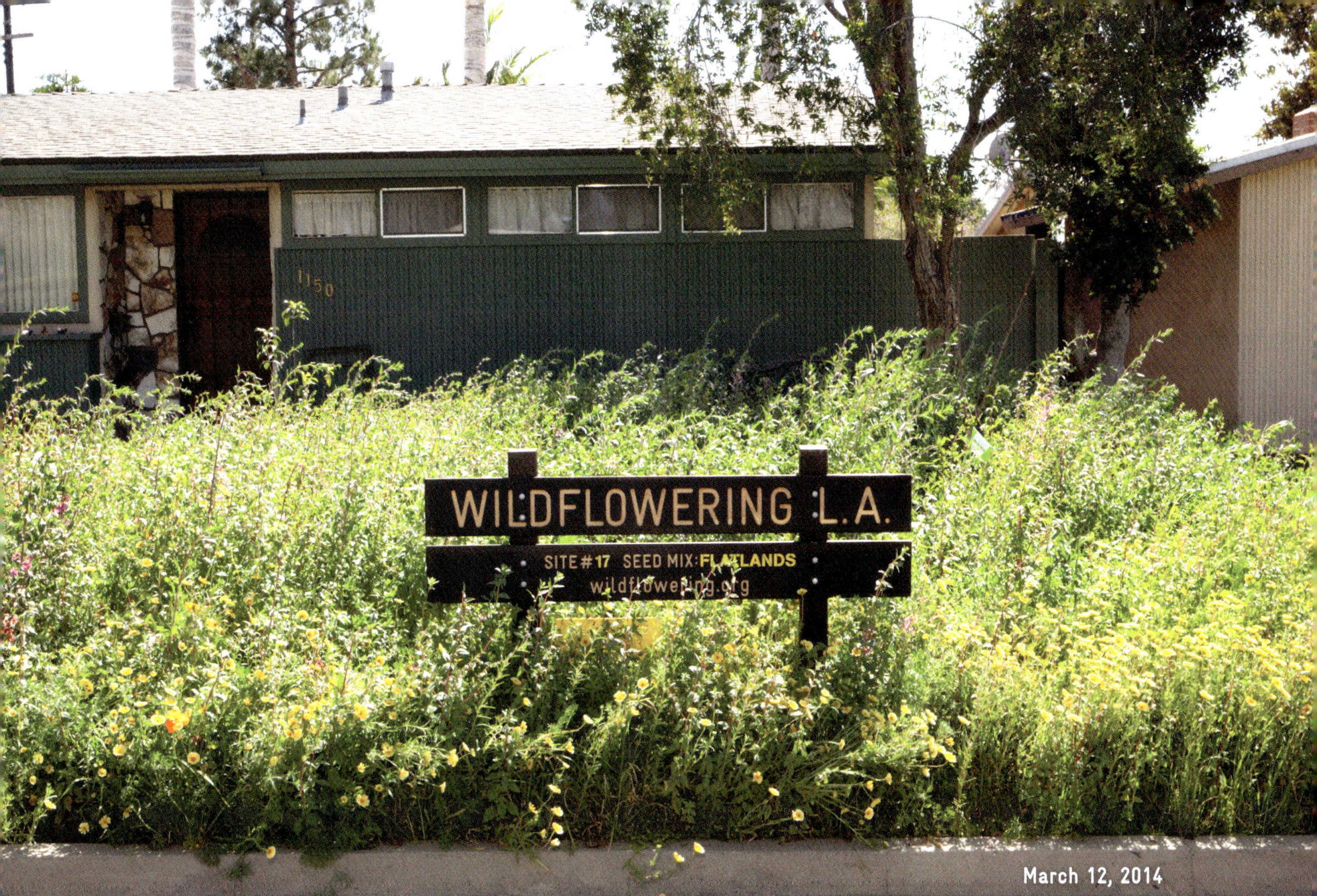

beyond. Cal Poly Pomona was using our site for sampling, and we will continue to provide our site to them and other institutions for educational purposes.

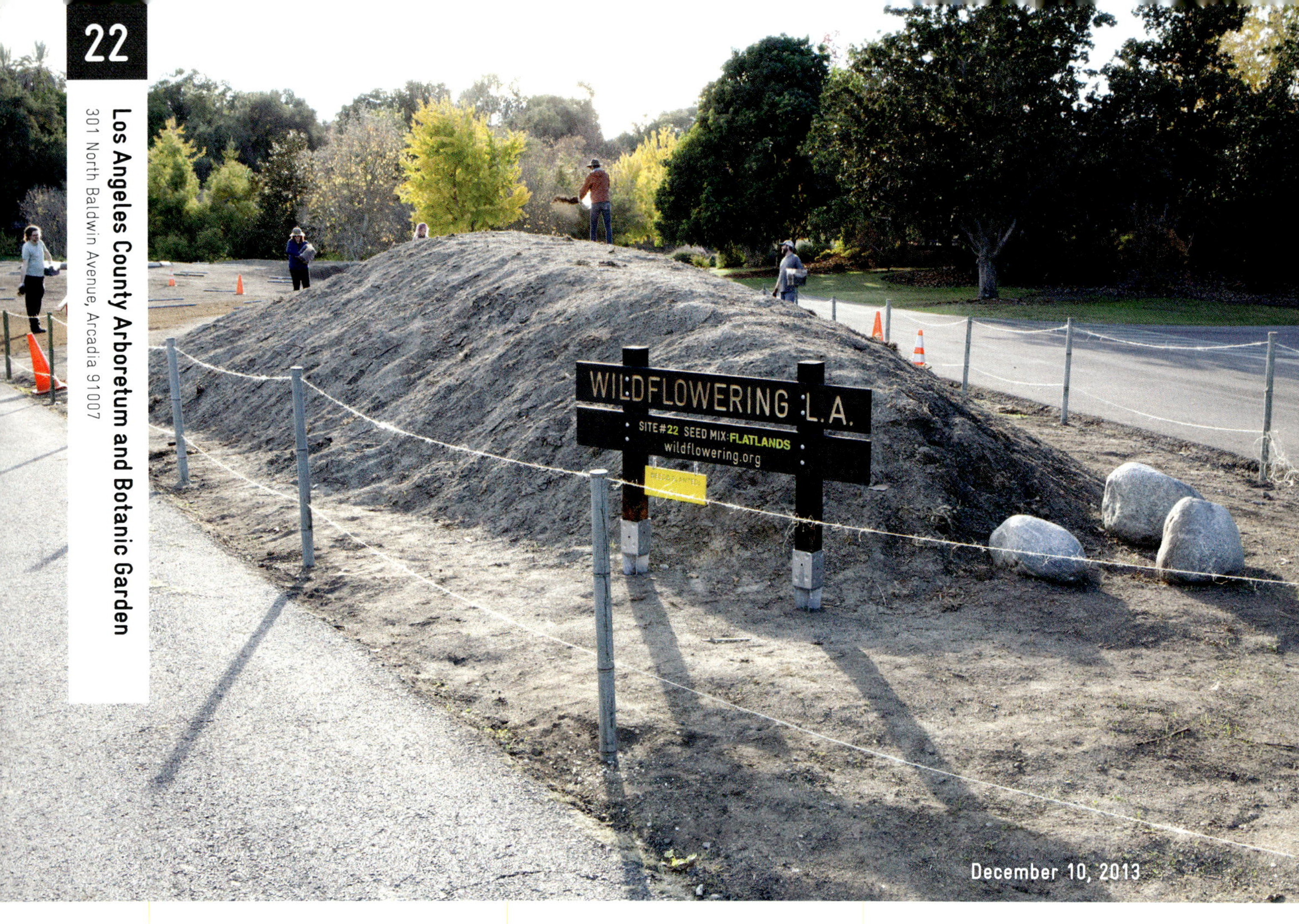

APR 8 We are seeing unprecedented numbers of pollinators and native birds and caterpillars… the meadow is spectacular! The bees are on the *Layia* (Tidy Tips) in the morning and the California Poppy in the afternoon. But there are birds — goldfinches and hummers — all day long, and mountain bluebirds in the afternoon. I think we're still a week or two away from peaking.

APR 15 One group among the many volunteers that worked on the site is a special education Adult Transition Program, for students ages 18-22, in Monrovia Unified School District. They have been very involved in the garden and take huge pride in having contributed to the bloom.

JUN 12 The site is still quite beautiful with a few California Poppy, Winecup Clarkia, and Elegant Clarkia continuing to bloom. In the future, this site will feature wildflowers interspersed with varying foodscapes.

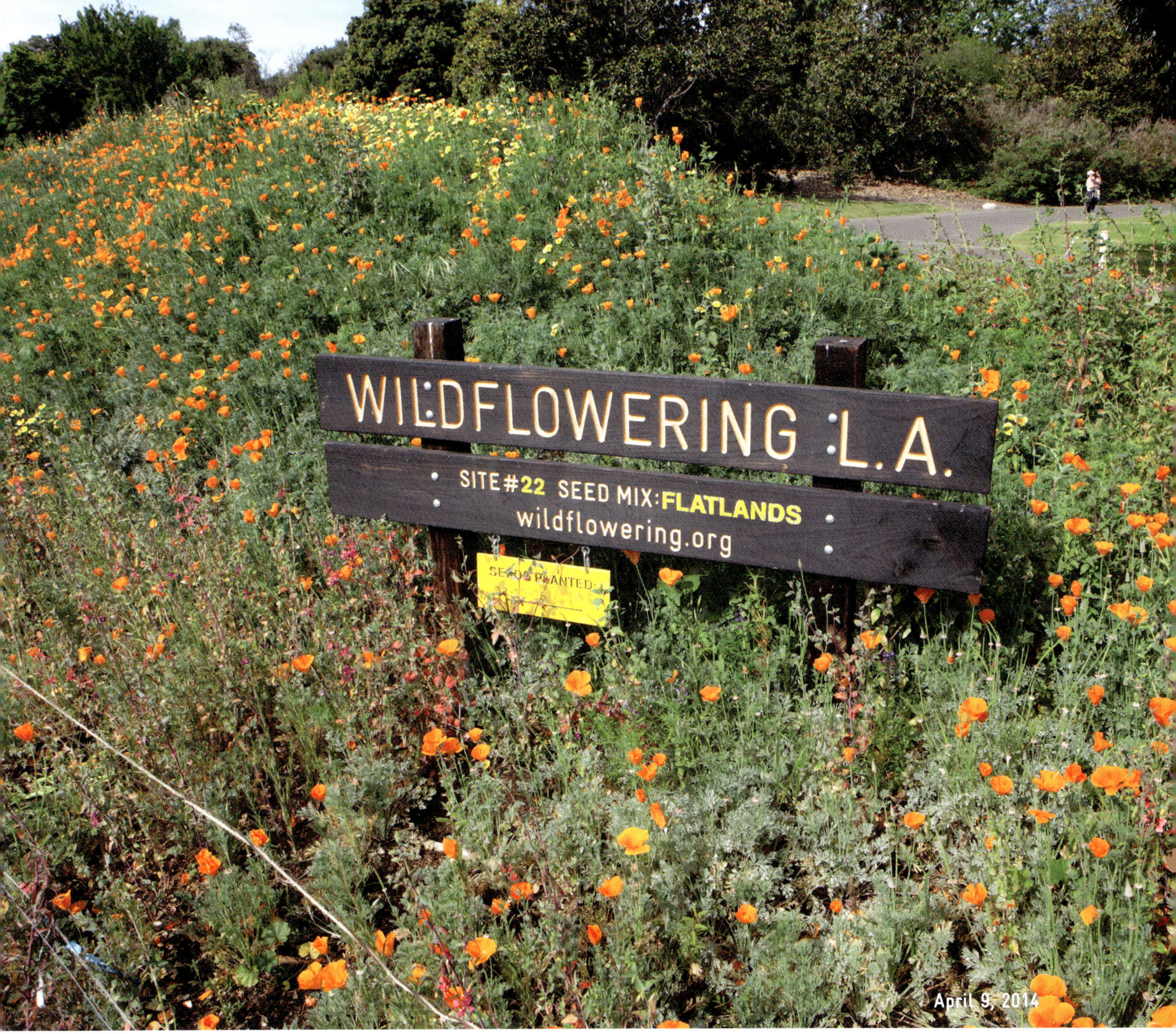

A one-acre site at the Los Angeles County Arboretum and Botanic Garden featured a sloping hügelkultur mound built from organic biomass that fed the soil to enhance the bloom.

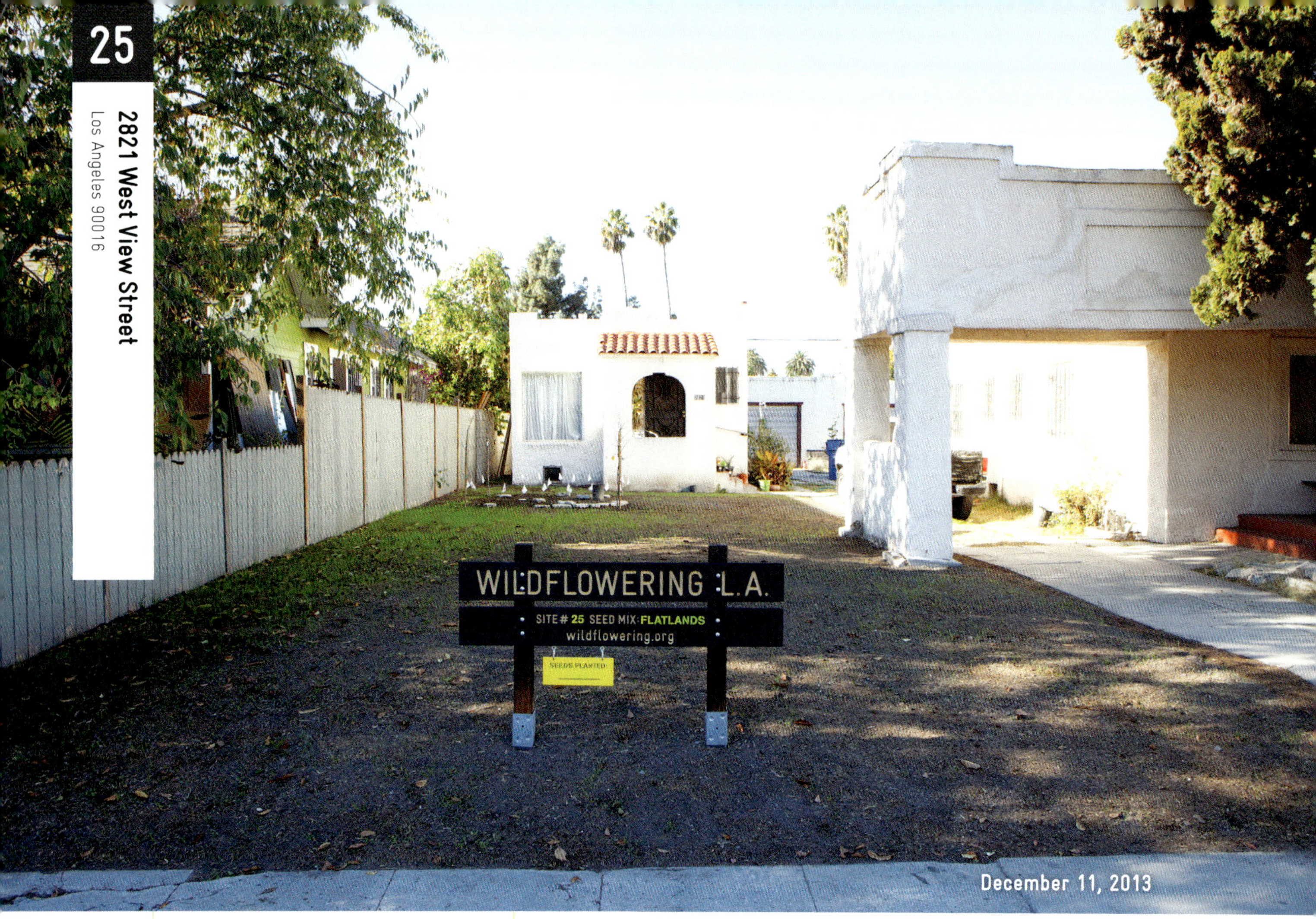

MAY 18 My site remains in bloom and going decently strong. I've got browning of course, but it is still worth visiting. This has been an amazing experience and an educational one as well, showing the neighborhood and city the potential beauty of low-water, native gardens. I'm in the landscape design field and have found that often the question with using these native and low-water alternatives is not how they will look at their peak, but rather what happens the rest of the year and the year after that.

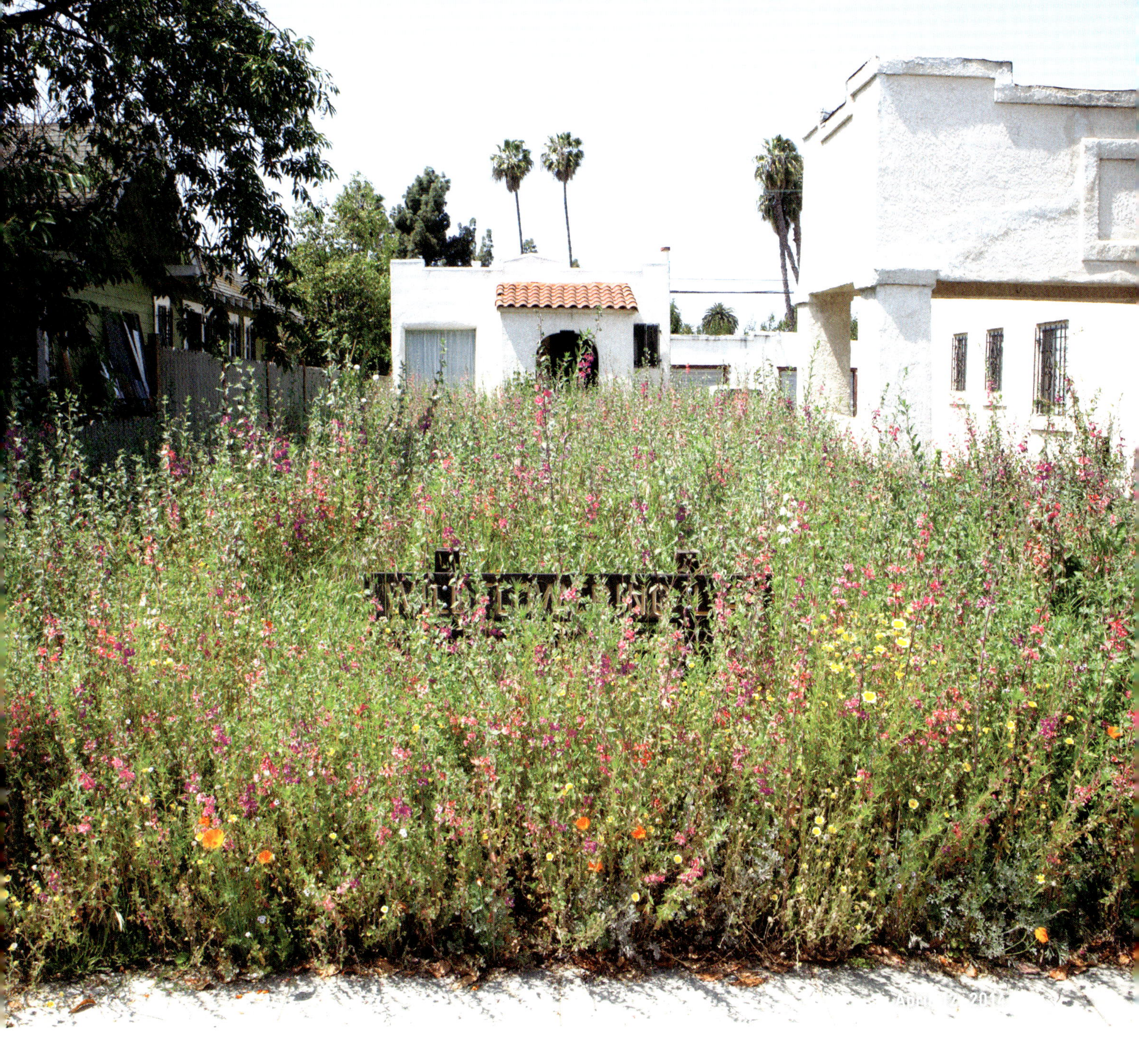

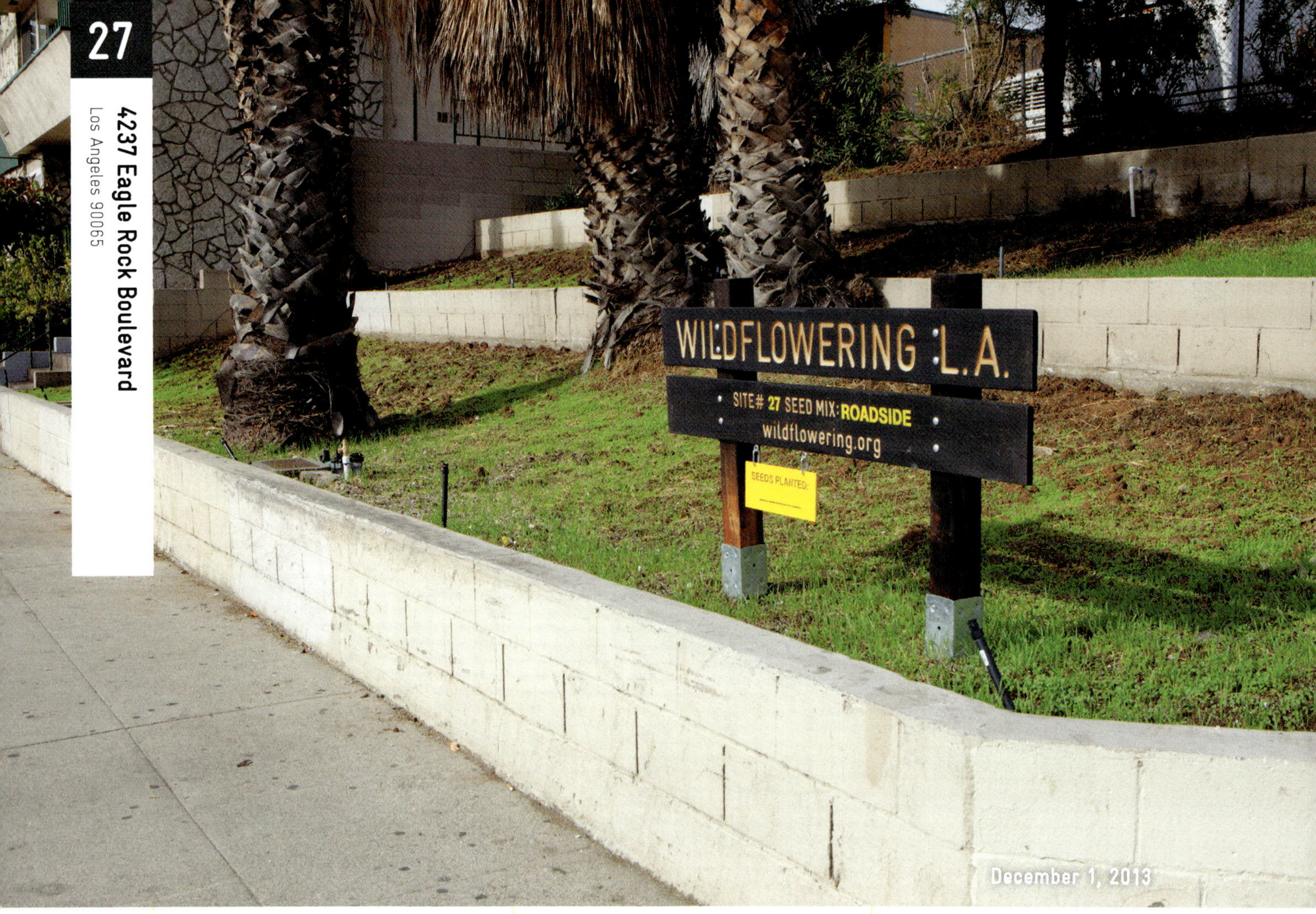

DEC 17 Our sprouts are coming in strong over in Eagle Rock. Excited to be part of the *Wildflowering L.A.* project!

JAN 8 The first of our wildflowers are beginning to bloom!

MAR 10 Our site is in full bloom with a wide variety of colorful Lupine and Elegant Clarkia. I'm guessing we will be at peak next week or the week after. The right side of the property still needs to come in just a tad. We have been documenting the process from planting to bloom on Facebook using the hashtag #wildfloweringla.

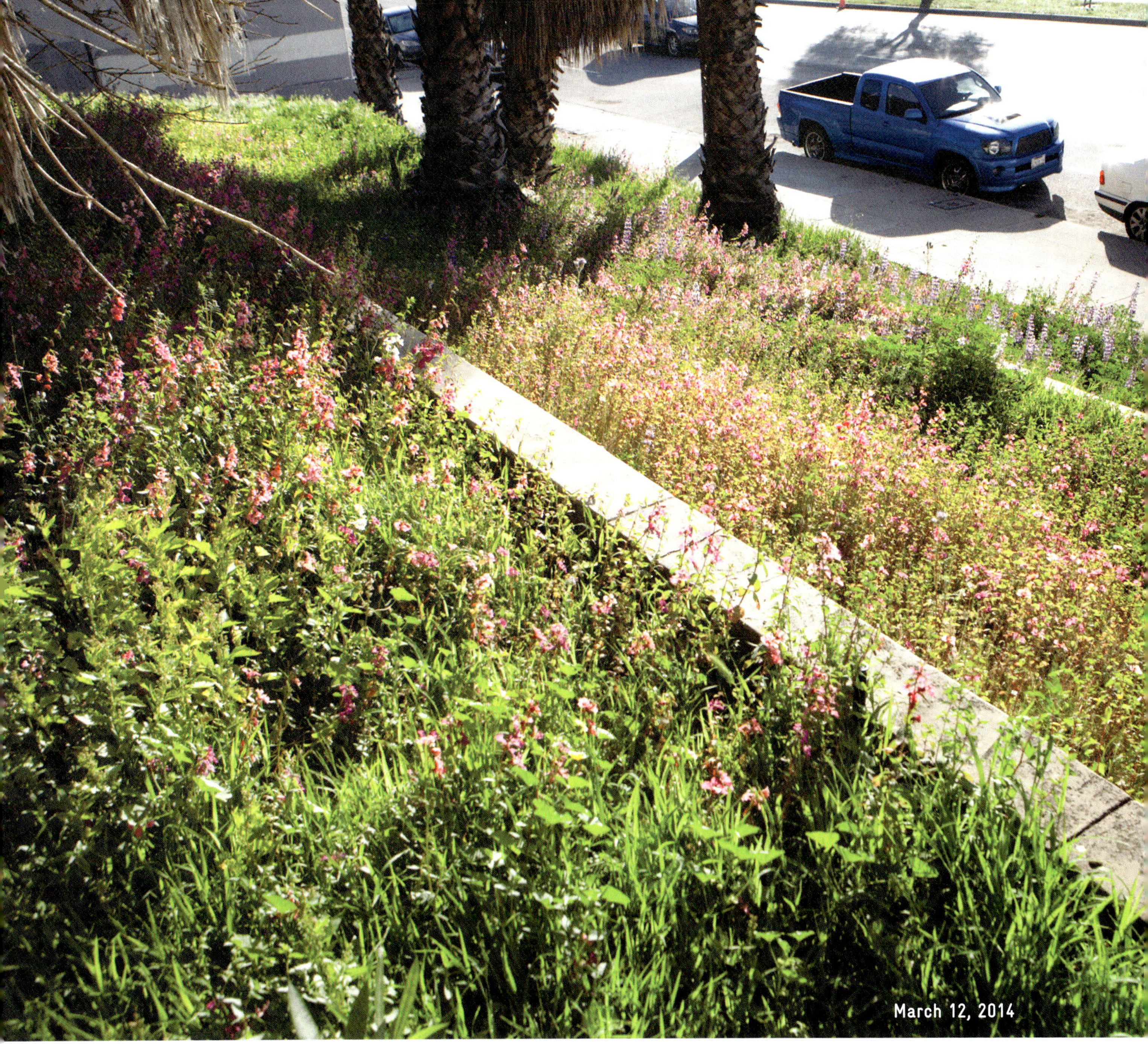

March 12, 2014

3847 DuRay Place
Los Angeles 90008

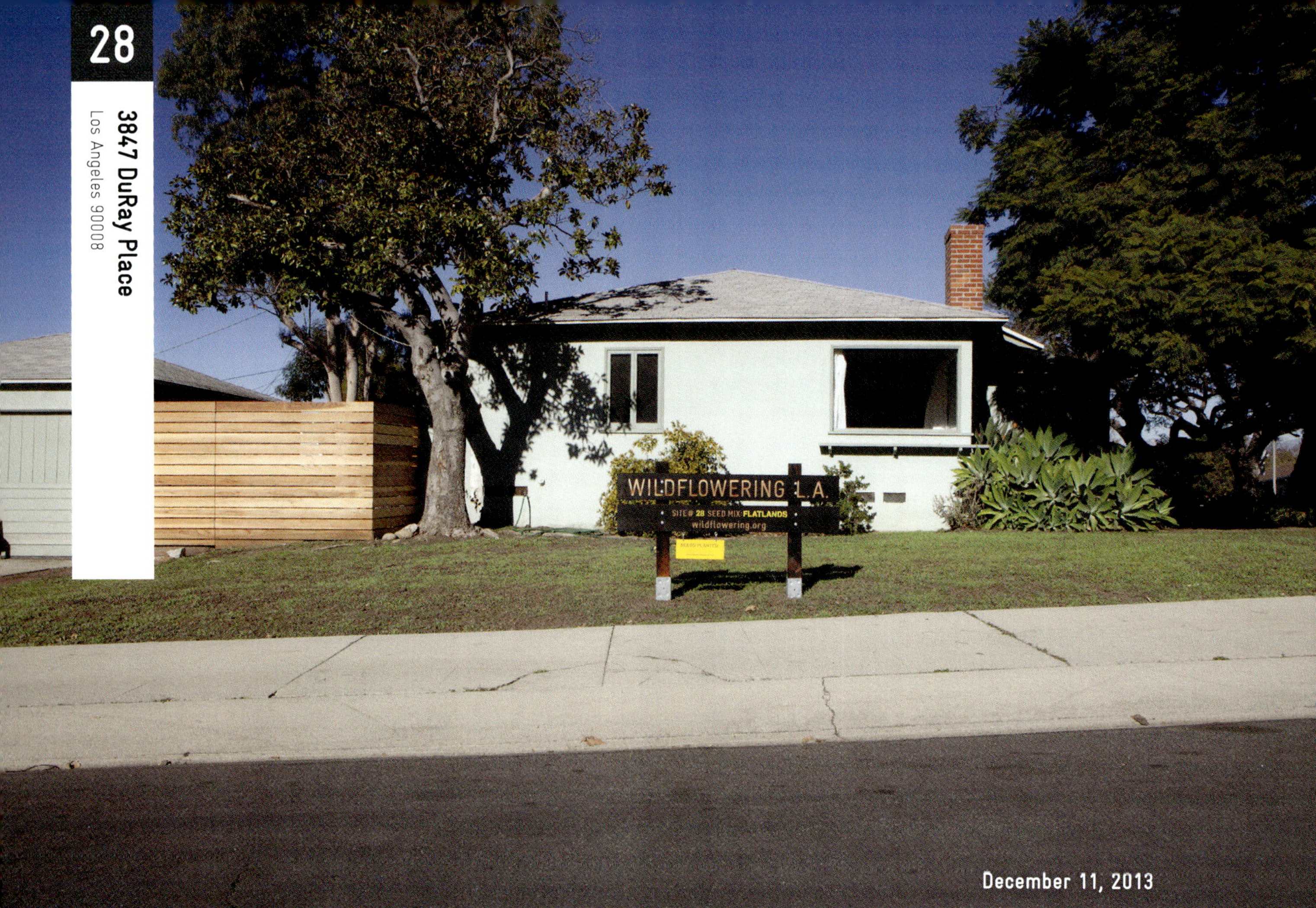

DEC 11 The project has resulted in many good conversations. People in the neighborhood are calling each other and asking about it. Someone even asked me to come out of the house yesterday to talk about the project! We discuss native plants and the necessity of them for wildlife to continue to exist. People seem to have reservations about doing the work to take out the grass, but love the idea. A woman walked by yesterday and told me she can't wait until it blooms.

FEB 9 Tidy Tips are doing nicely. When the Tidy Tips dry out, I will start the first round of seed collecting for next year. I'm enjoying this project immensely as are the bees.

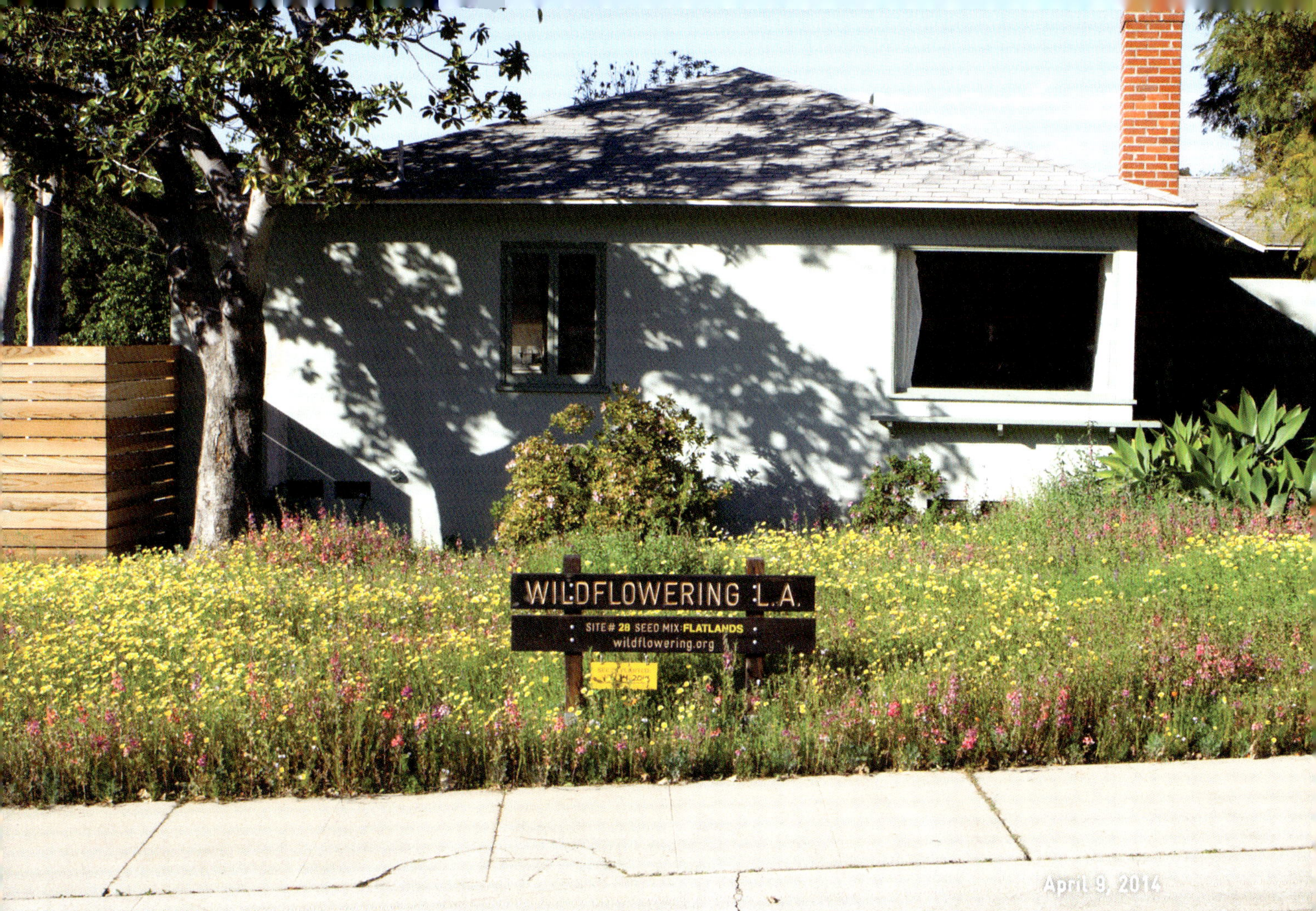

MAR 9 All the colors are starting to come in, except for the Purple Needlegrass and White Yarrow.

APR 9 The site is a little past peak but there are a lot of bees using it in the morning.

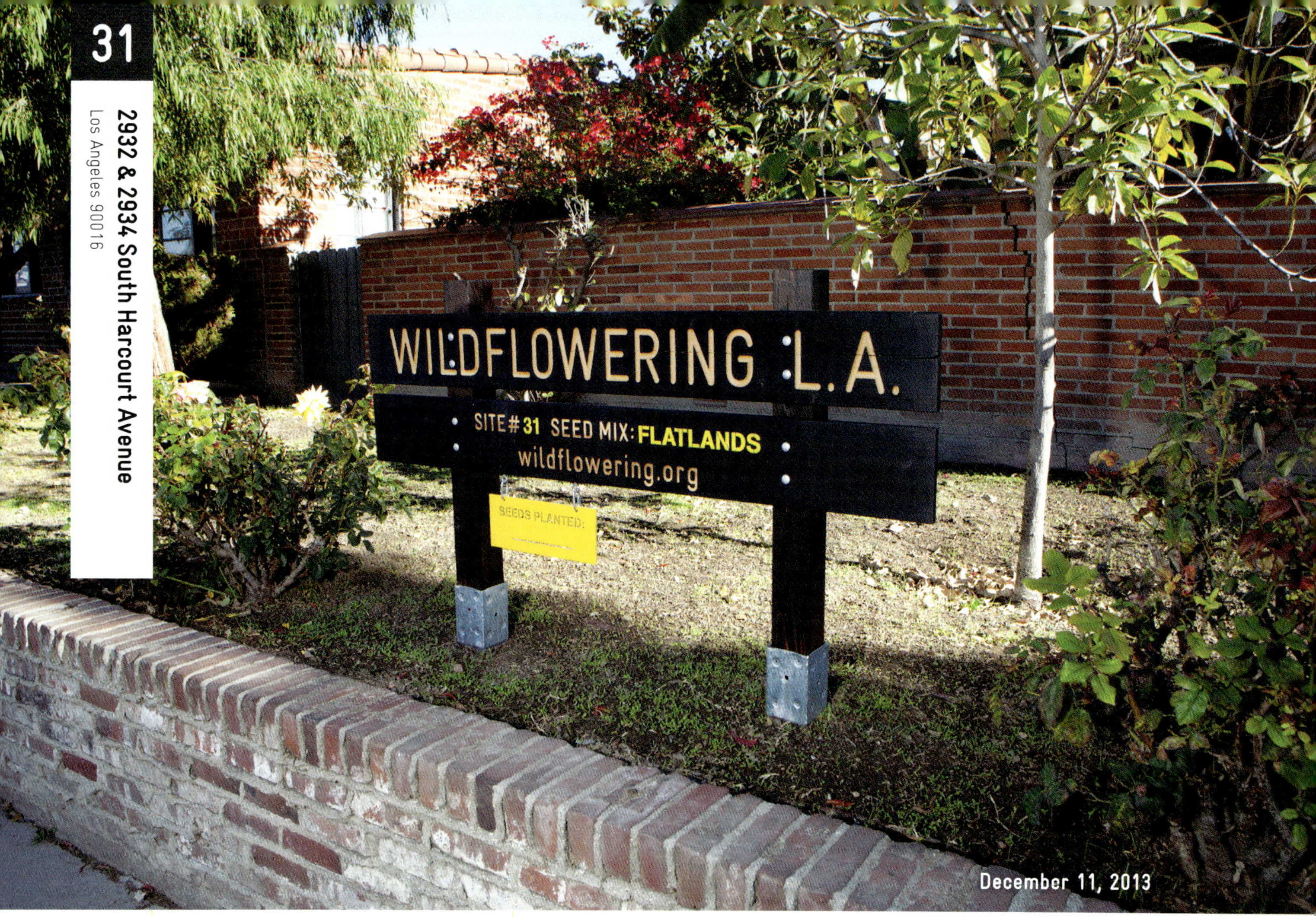

MAR 10 The flowers were kind of tramped down by the recent rain and haven't really sprung back. I think they're peaking very soon — just saw my second flower species and color today.

MAY 12 The bottom half looks pretty dried out, and is better close-up from the side-walk than from the street. Still blooming though!

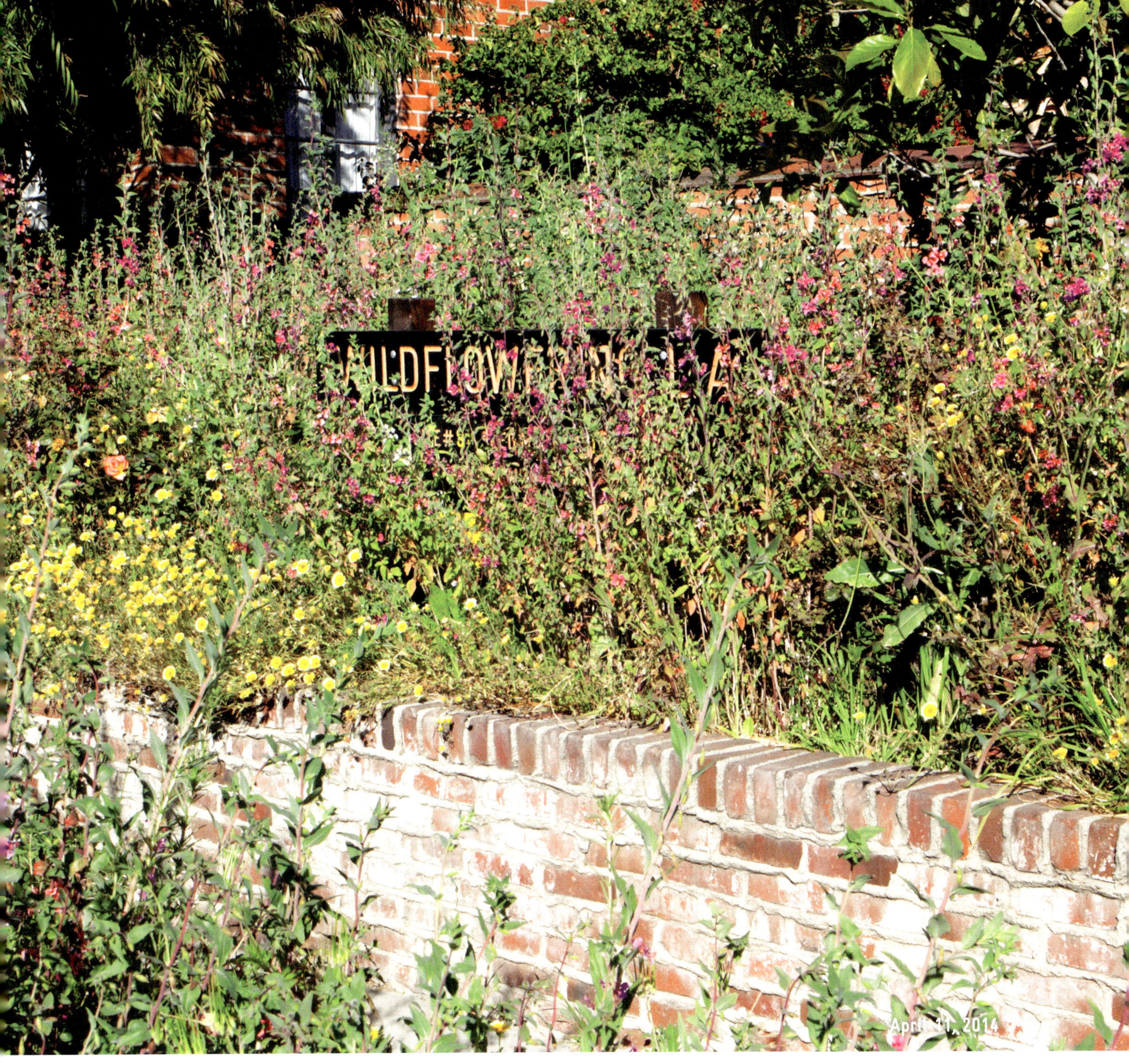
WILDFLOWERING L.A.
April 11, 2014

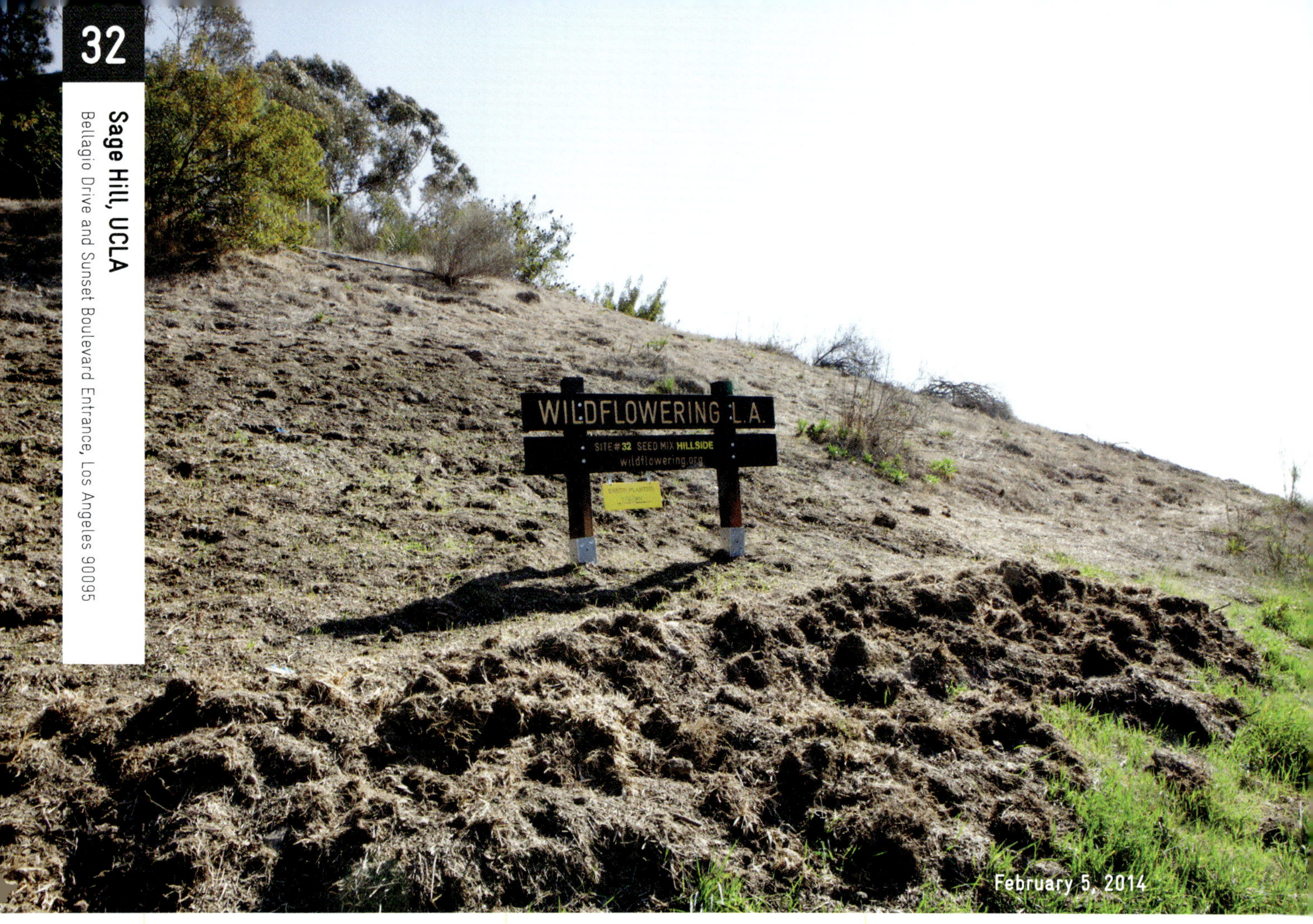

MAR 18 We planted in late January, so no blossoms yet but lots of seedlings. We expect to see some blossoms in two weeks.

APR 23 UCLA as a site has had a huge impact on kids, parents, and teachers at the Kreiger Childcare Center as well as a big impact on the undergraduate students who worked on the site directly! We will plant a larger area next year.

MAY 14 Because we planted late, there are still a number of things blooming. The *Clarkia unguic-ulata* (Elegant Clarkia) is coming in now and I will give Site #32 one last deep watering tomorrow.

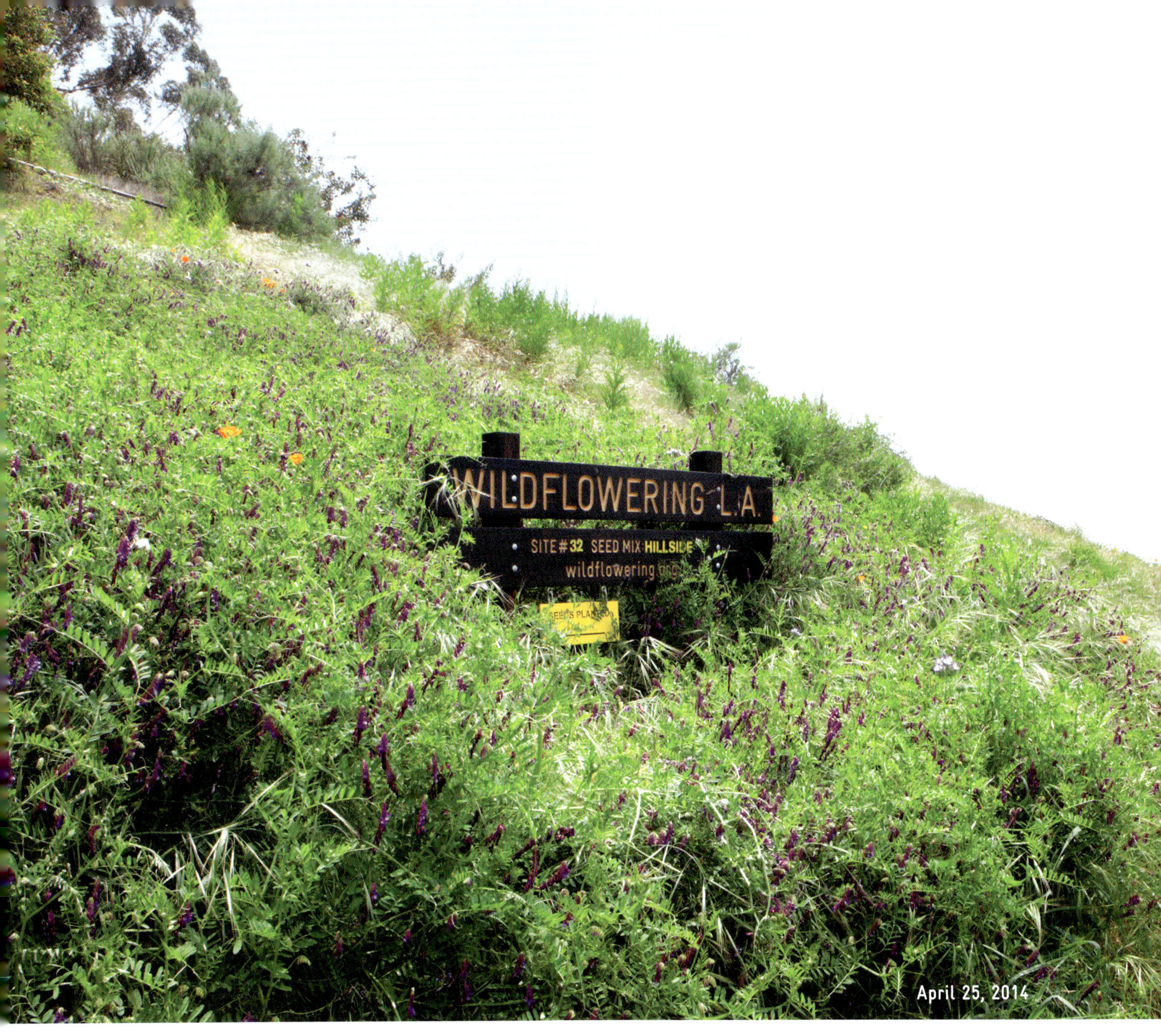

Planted by UCLA Department of Geography students at Sage Hill, a native area on the
UCLA campus.

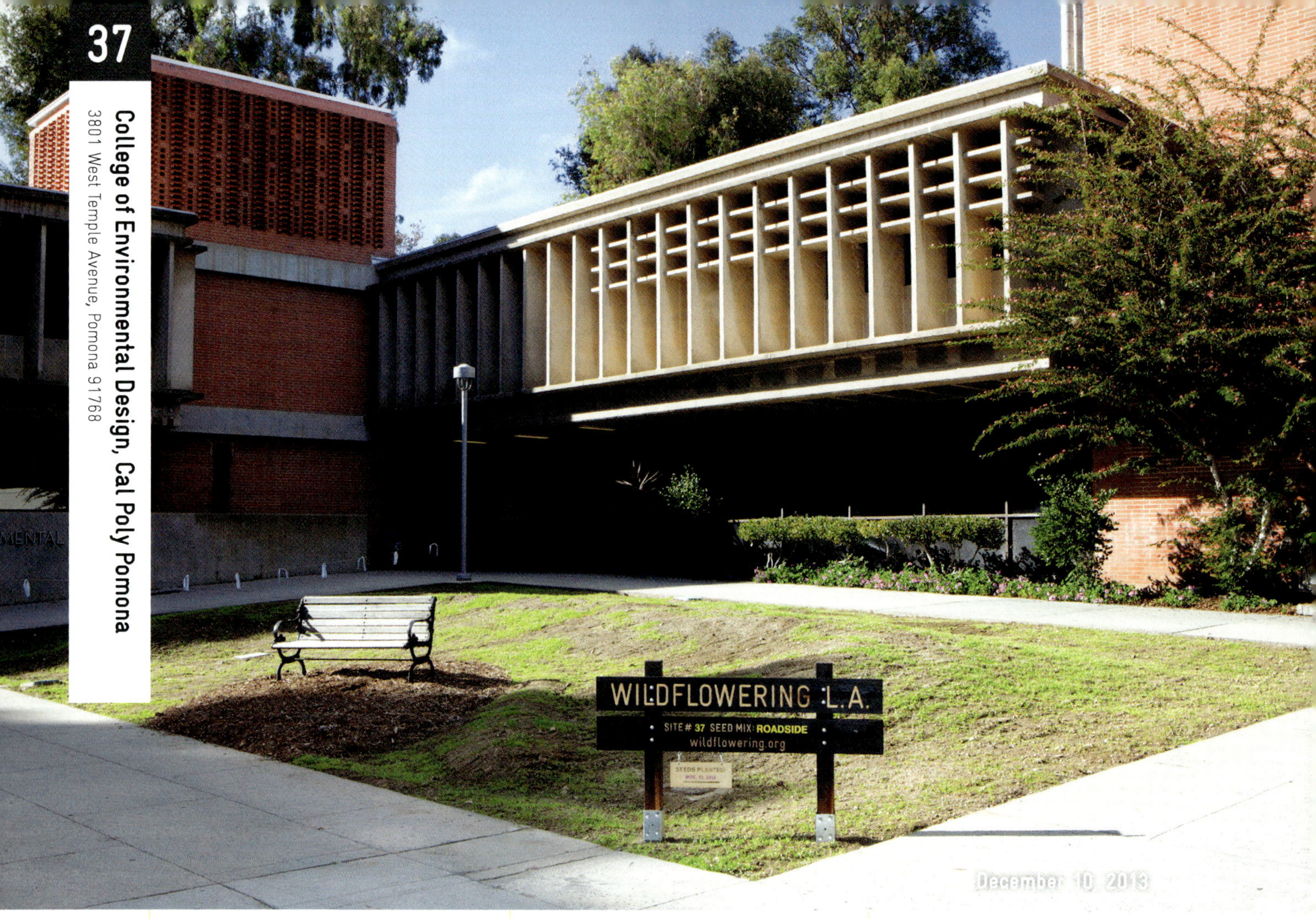

FEB 28 Site #37 is in full bloom now. I would assume Cal Poly Pomona will have an early peak with the unavoidable heat of the Pomona Valley. It gets many, many comments — especially from folks who know how dull it was before with the lawn.

APR 10 The meadow is bringing a great deal of joy to the campus community. A small series of pressed flowers was done by one of the students, and we have taken time-lapse images from site preparation to sowing to waiting to bloom and beyond.

JUN 13 The wildflowers are pretty brown now. The campus' facilities department has been taking "concerned" phone calls about the site. It is really challenging people now that the obvious "prettiness" has faded and the beautiful process of this California landscape has really emerged. I also appreciate the fact that the crews who plant turf and annual color now have to explain this process.

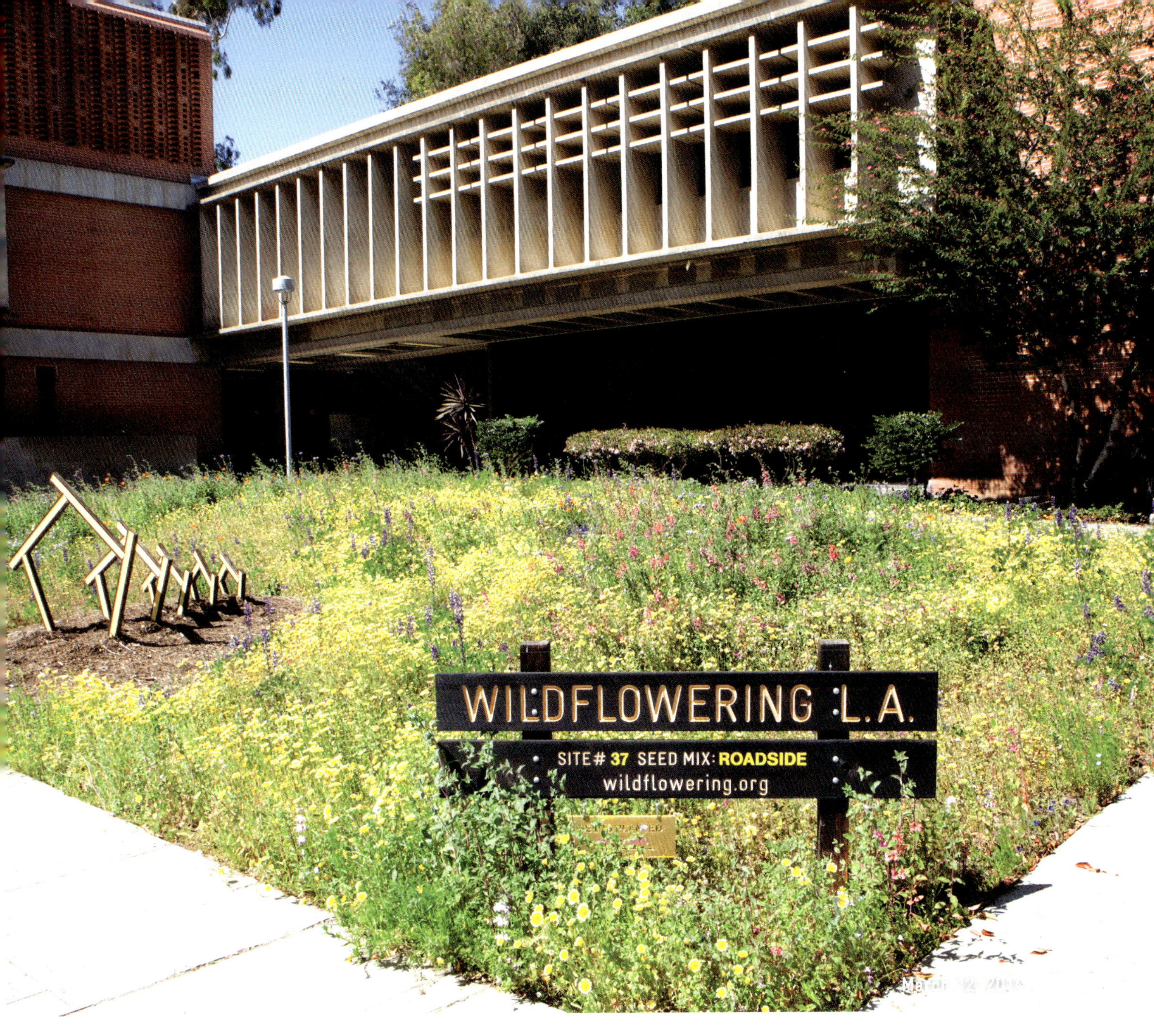

Planted by students and faculty of Cal Poly Pomona.

Carthay Center Elementary School
6351 West Olympic Boulevard, Los Angeles 90048

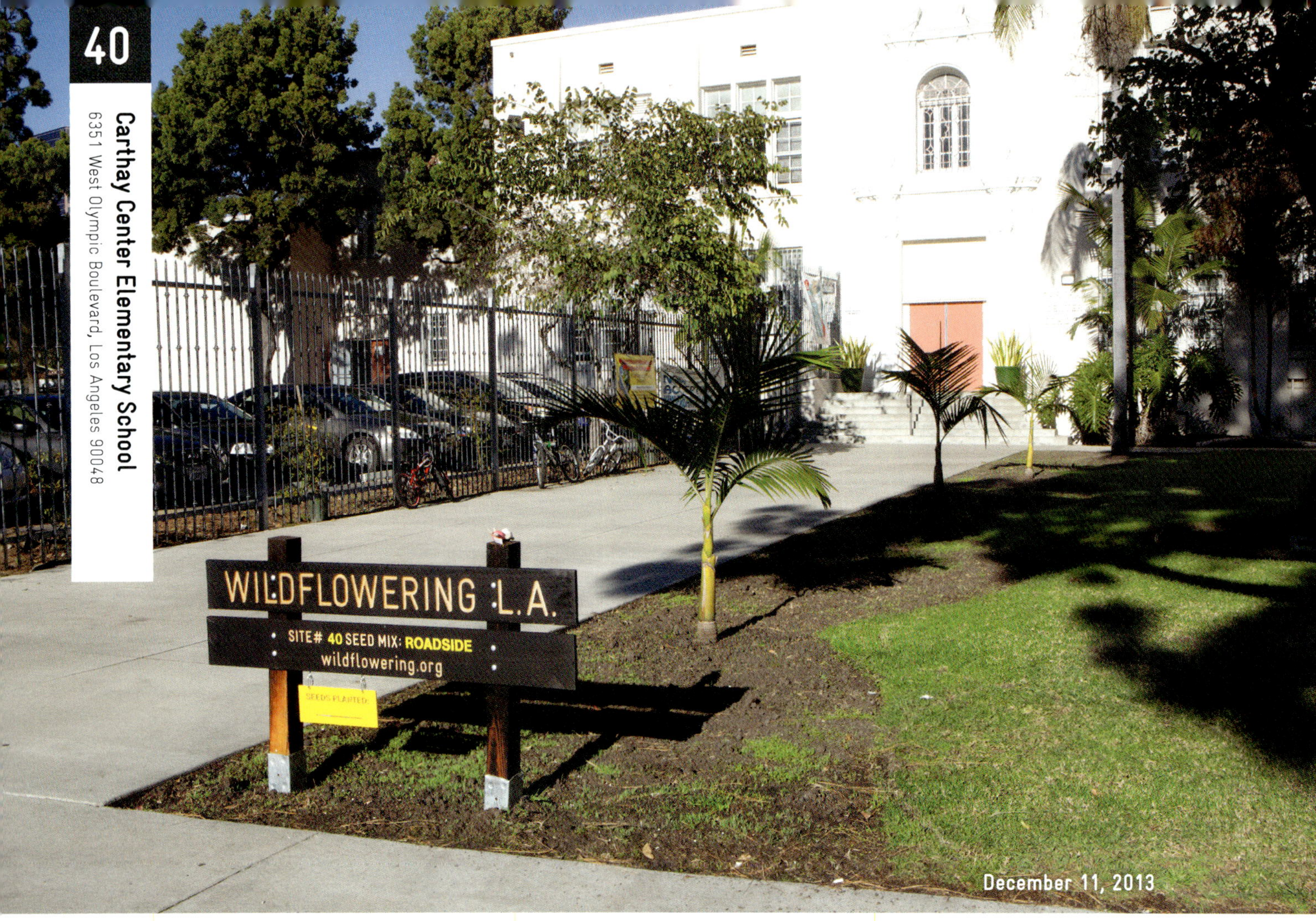

December 11, 2013

MAR 13 We planted two beds with our 1st graders — one is off-the-hook good! I would estimate peak time as nearly now.

APR 10 1st graders in Ms. Finn's class have looked at and investigated the blooms with magnifying glasses, and other students have created beautiful drawings about the bloom. Older students have researched the artist and written letters — we'd love to share these all for the exhibit!

MAY 12 Carthay Center's site is also past prime but still looking good — tall Clarkia and California Poppy — beautiful. We will begin our seed harvest this Sunday. Carthay Center Elementary School is grateful to have been included in *Wildflowering L.A.* It transformed the entrance — and feeling as one enters — the front of our school. Such a simple and powerful idea that brought families together digging

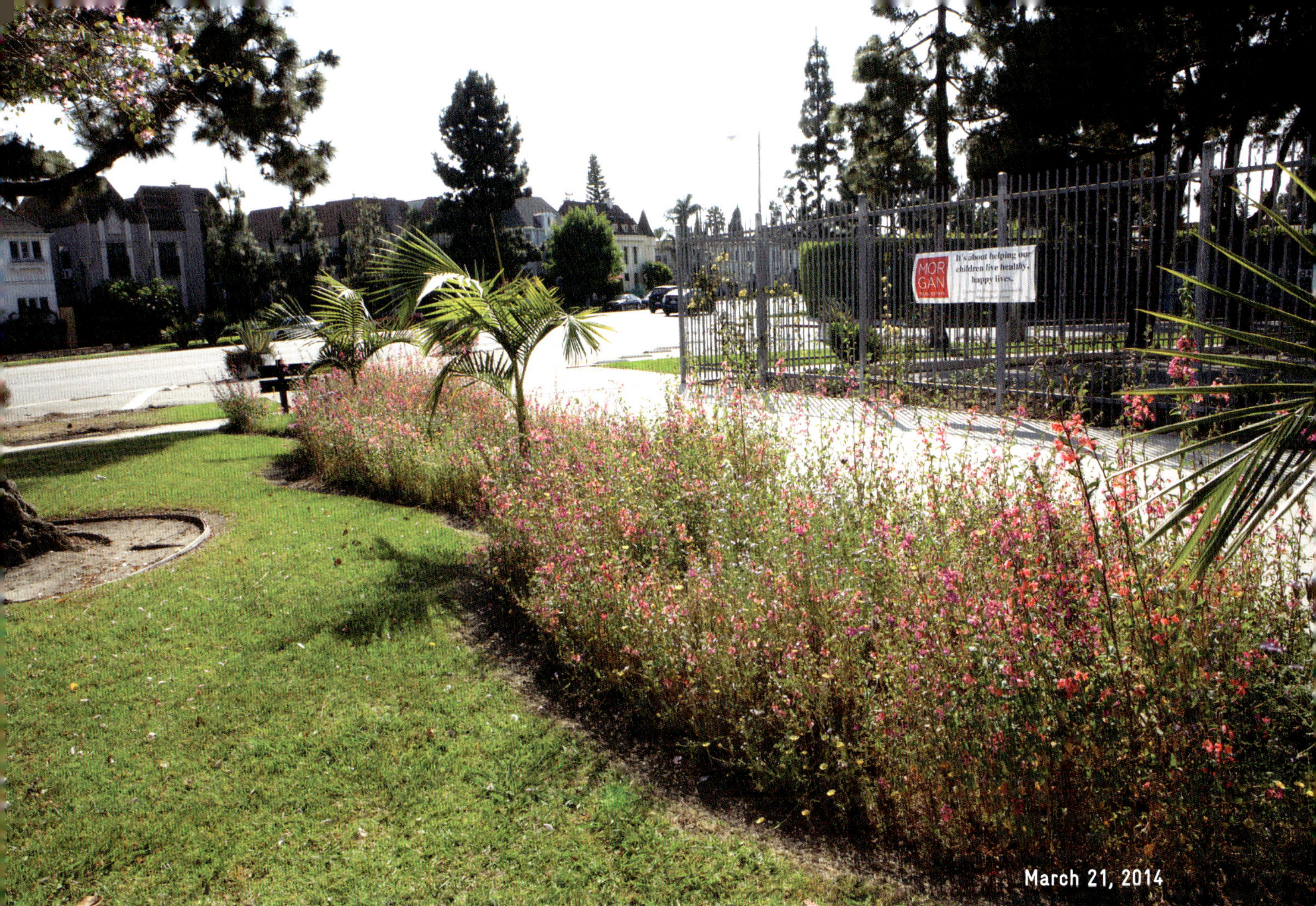

out the lawn. Students also learned how native plants help attract pollinators to our edible garden. But, more than anything, I hope this project helps our community think differently about landscape — especially as we let our flowers go to seed and regenerate next year, and the next, and the next...

 Our flowers still look beautiful as they go to seed.

Planted by students, parents, and teachers of Carthay Center Elementary School.

5430 Sanchez Drive
Los Angeles 90008

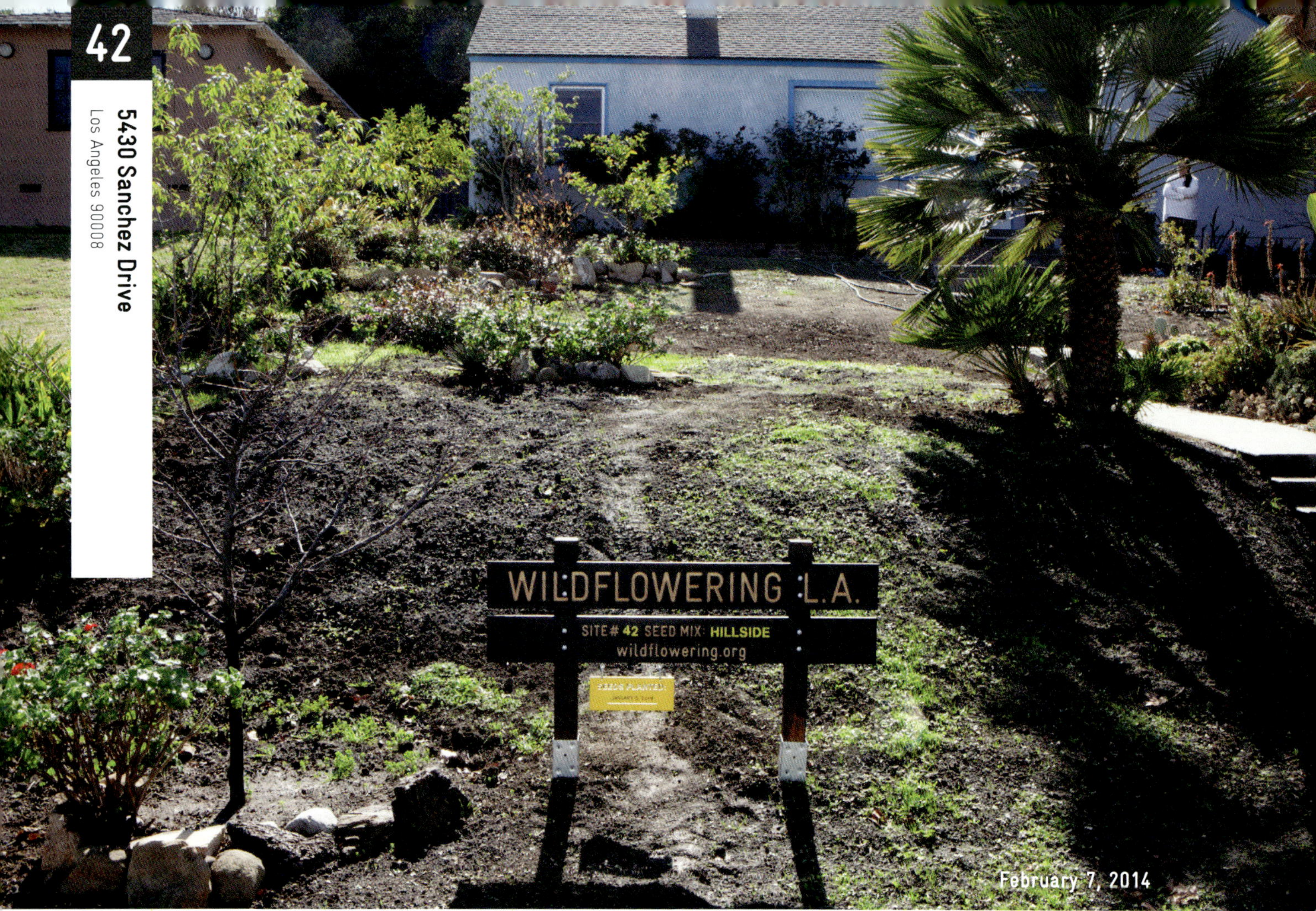

DEC 30 My husband turned over all the soil to get rid of the weeds that were there, and it looks ready for sowing the seed for wildflowers!

JAN 8 We have the seeds. They are planted and we are watering!

MAR 11 Since we planted late (in December) I am guessing our site is about a month behind our neighbor's plot just down the street from us on DuRay, whose planting inspired us to take part.

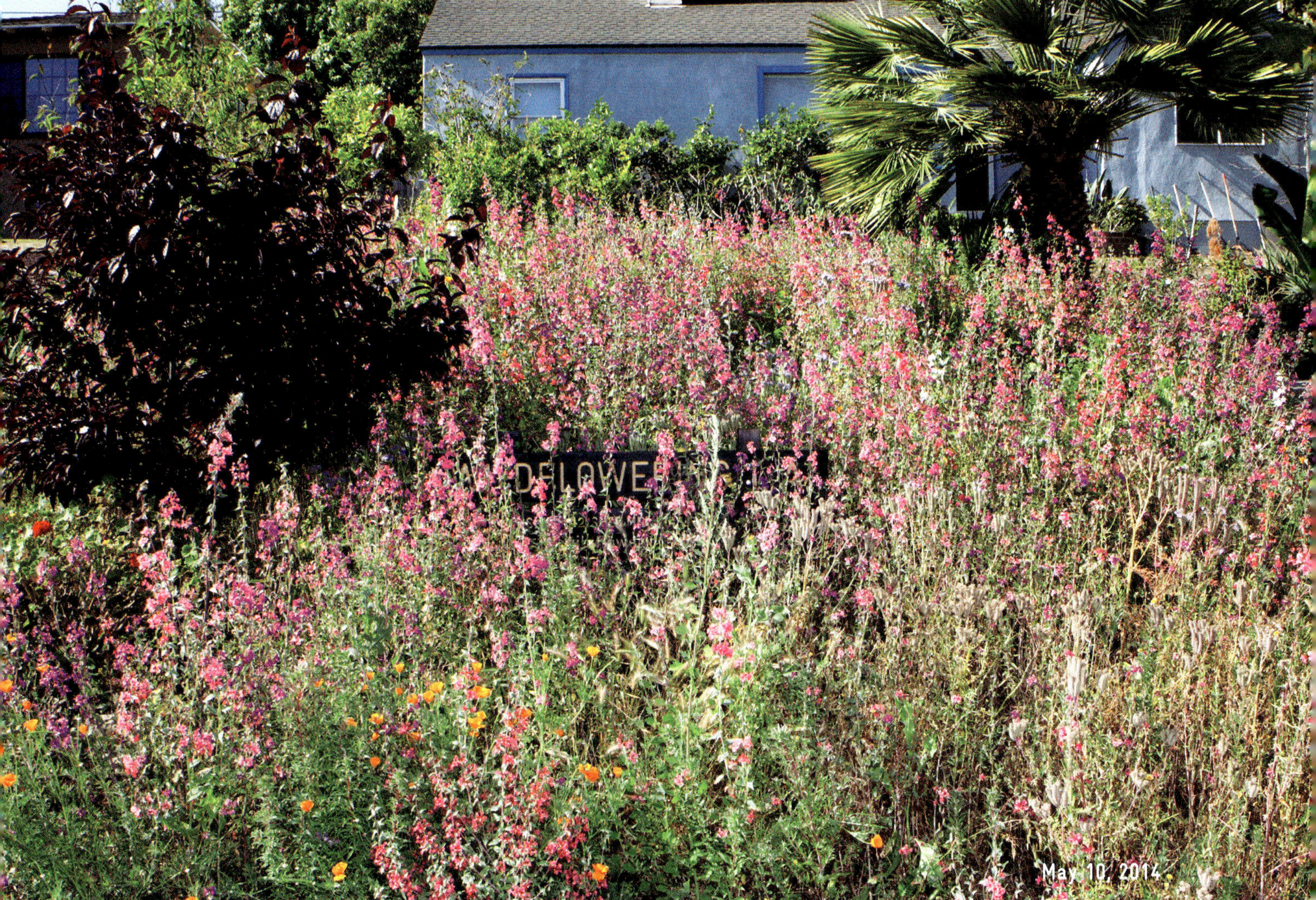

APR 20 In full bloom with tall, hardy, gorgeous Elegant Clarkia!

MAY 12 The wildflowers are looking a bit dry, but still pretty.

MAY 20 There are still blooms though there are many brown spots as well...though it looks kind of cool and wild with some color...everything looks very dry, though I have noticed small birds seem to be landing on the flowers... maybe eating the seeds?

478 East Avenue 28
Los Angeles 90031

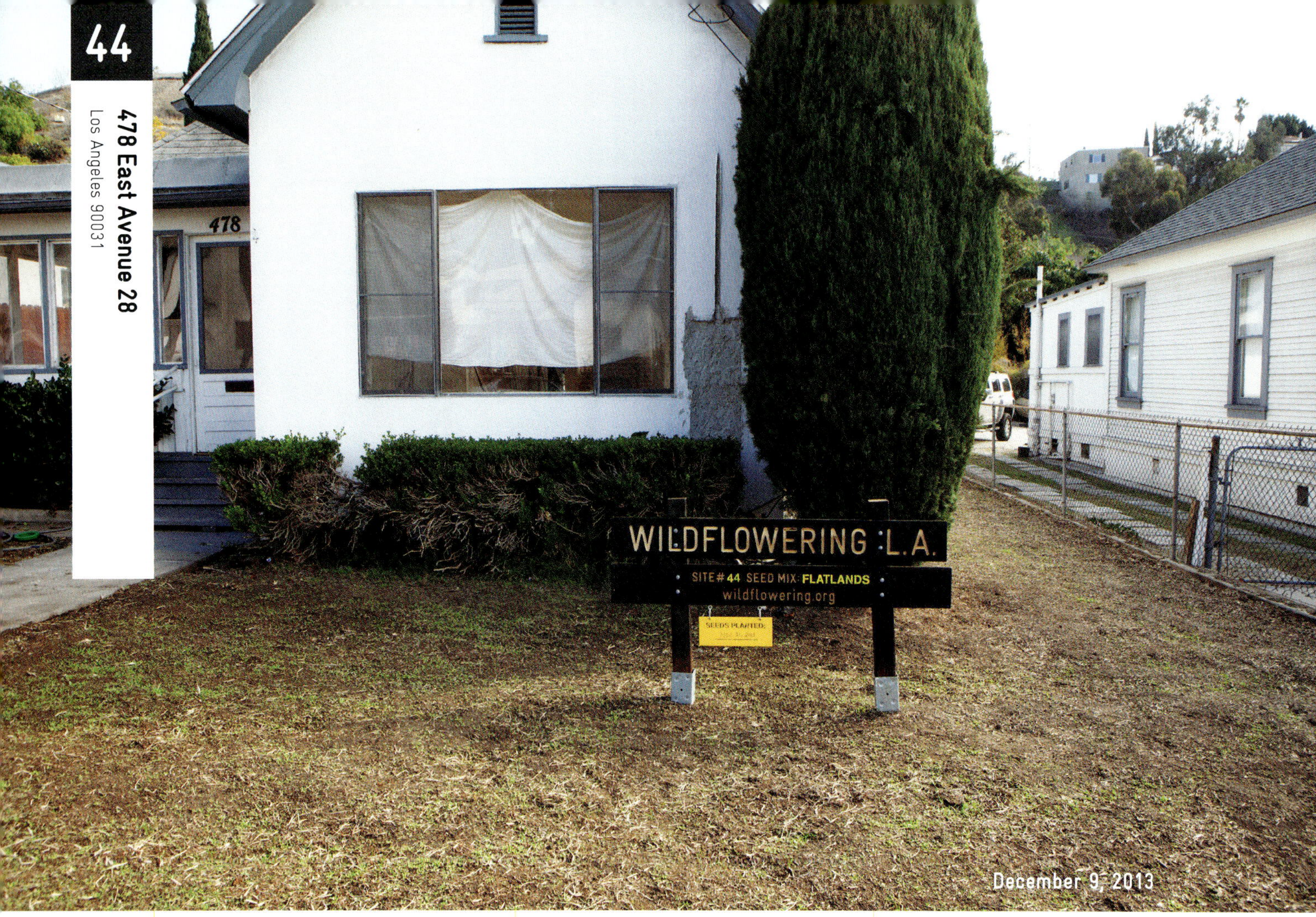

NOV 22 I finally got the seeds in yesterday after the auspicious day of rain! So far, so good. I get many people stopping by, asking about the sign and what's happening with the yard.

FEB 25 I need to research the weeds on our site. There are some things sprouting and I'm not sure whether they are an early stage of a wildflower or a true invasive weed.

FEB 28 Our site is really going nuts! The Tidy Tips are in full bloom and the foliage is really tall. We are having different flower peaks. Right now are Tidy Tips, but the Lupine are slowly starting to come out. The California Poppy seem to be getting full leaves in their patches, but no sign of blooms or petals yet. As it is, the Tidy Tips have gone crazy — I've got a field of 'em! Come on rain!

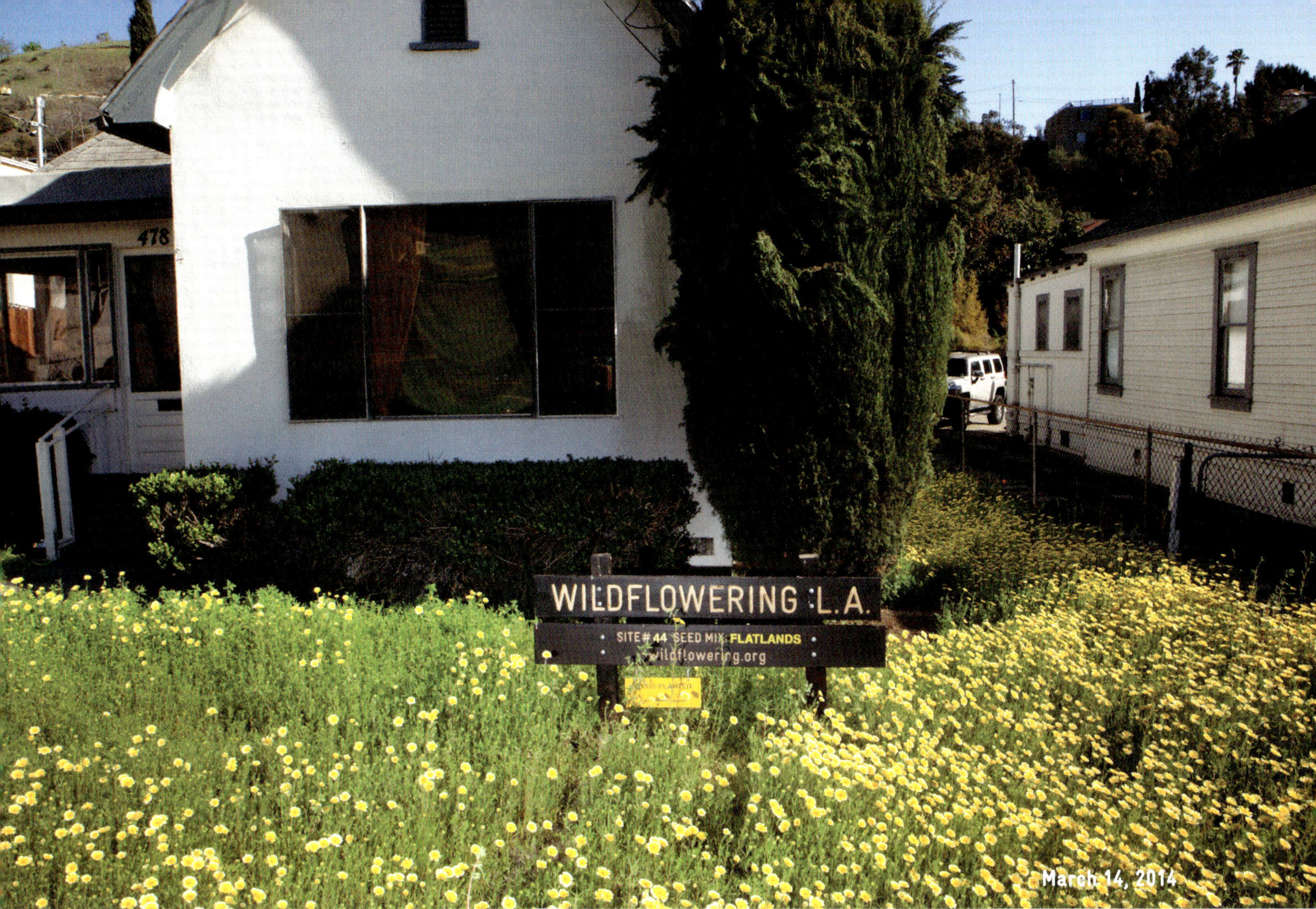

MAR 26 The two types of Clarkia are starting to go nuts!

MAY 12 Our site is definitely past peak, but there are still lots of Elegant Clarkia and clusters of California Poppy.

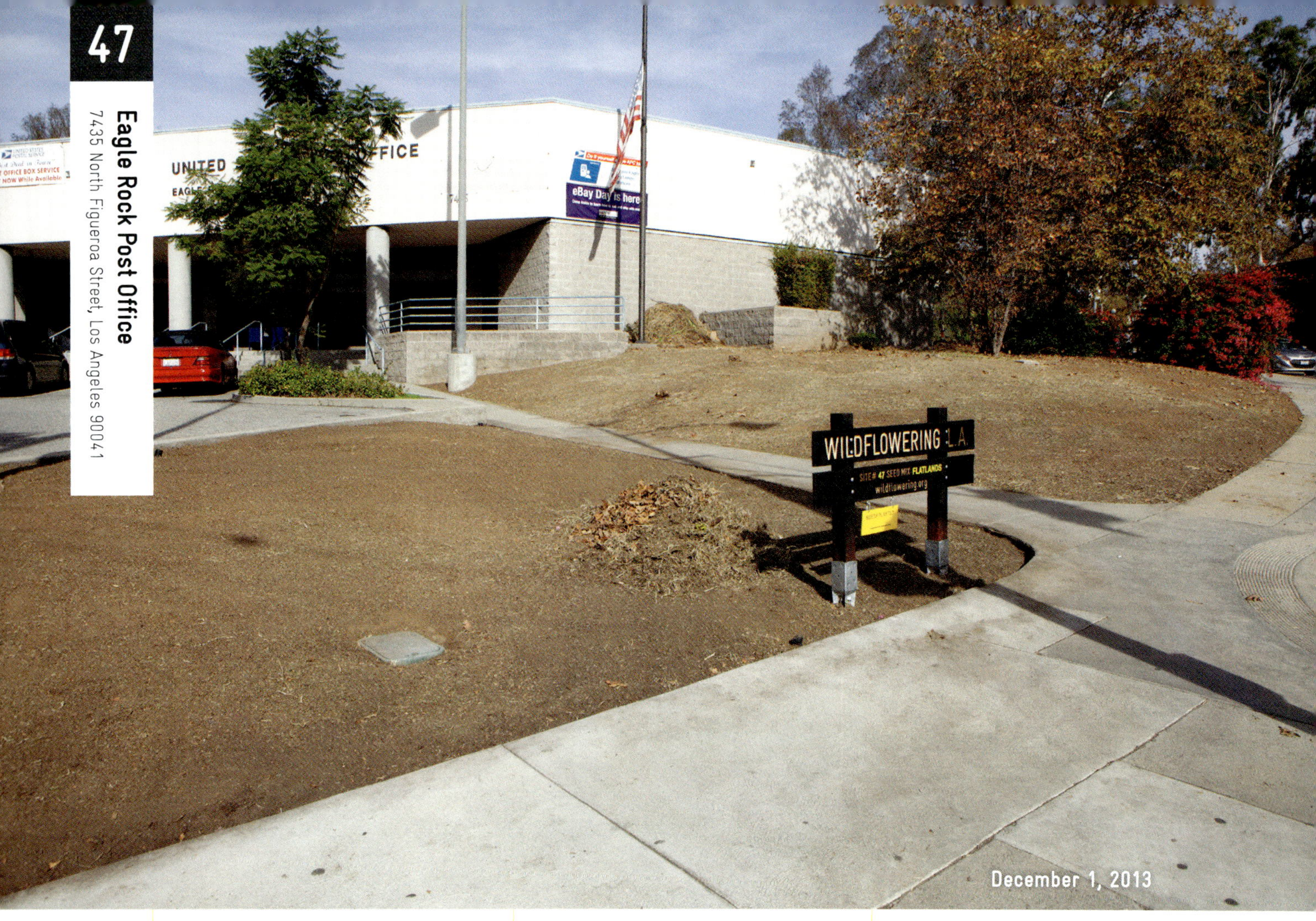

NOV 18 I have spoken to the post office staff. They are interested in the idea as long as the seed will be provided by *Wildflowering L.A.* and planted by volunteer labor (understandable given the current state of the USPS).

DEC 3 I will be getting out the last bits of lawn/weeds tomorrow and then the site will be quite pristine. To address the compacted soil, I purchased a gallon of Water-In (a product recommended by Lili Singer) and will be applying it as soon as the clearing is complete. This should help break the surface tension of the soil (which occurs when soil is baked under hot sun) and allows water to penetrate deeply into it.

DEC 20 I finally planted the seed at the site last Wednesday. Their irrigation installation process took longer than expected, but otherwise the post office has been most accommodating. I was even given a key to the irrigation controls so that I can monitor the site while the seeds are establishing.

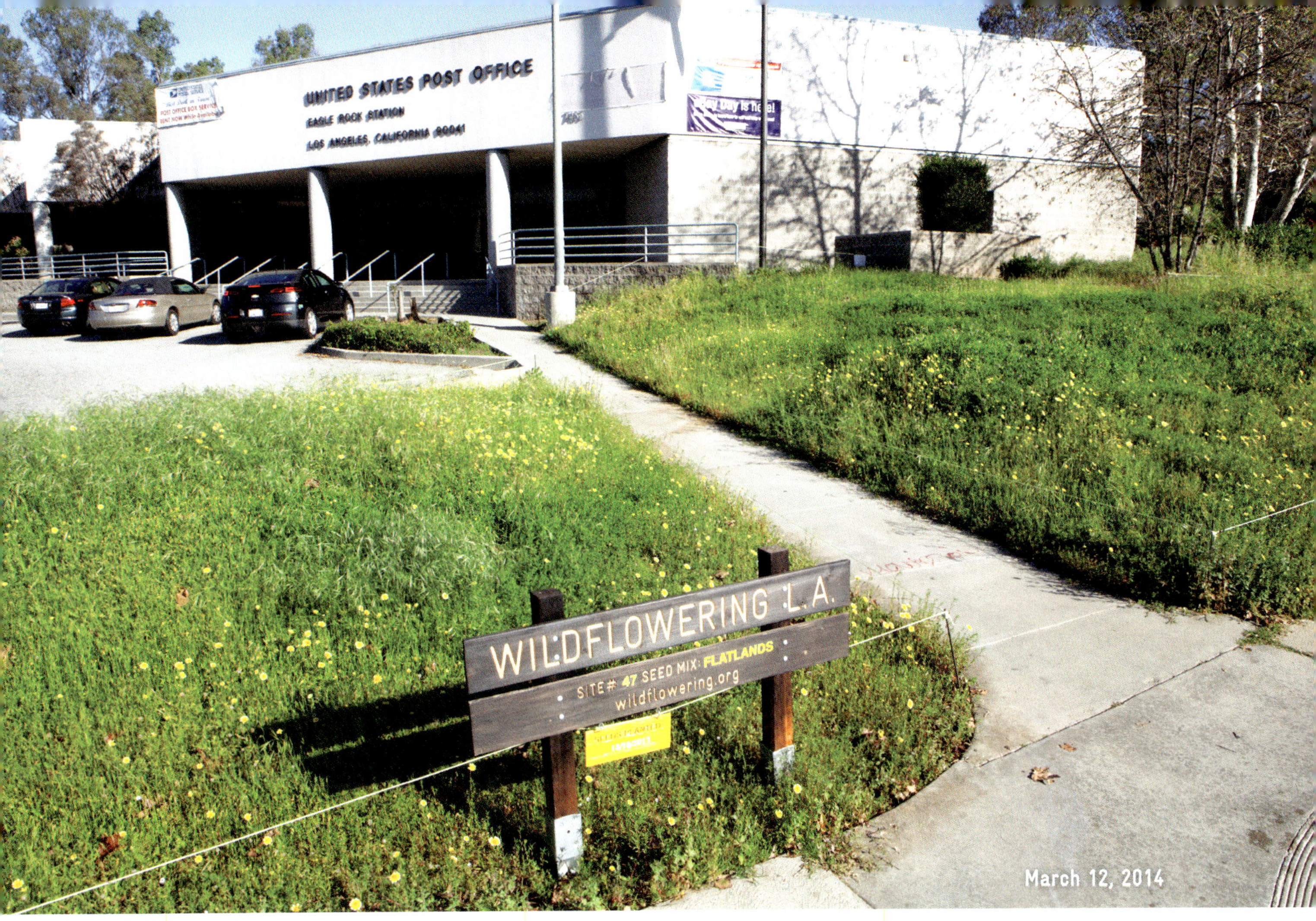

MAR 10 There are quite a few Tidy Tips blooming as well as scant Bird's-Eye Gilia and Lupine, among the unfortunate weeds. There are a good number of Elegant and Winecup Clarkia that have yet to produce buds but they should provide a decent display in about one month, in early April.

MAR 20 I am disheartened to report that a maintenance crew unexpectedly mowed down 75% of the wildflower field today. I received no notice about it. The only bit that remains is about 500 square feet surrounding the sign. There were many weeds to be sure but there were so many Clarkia that had set buds amongst them and many Tidy Tips in the area that was destroyed.

MAY 18 I do hope something more will come of the *Wildflowering L.A.* effort at the Eagle Rock Post Office site. It has been so instructive and enlightening on many levels.

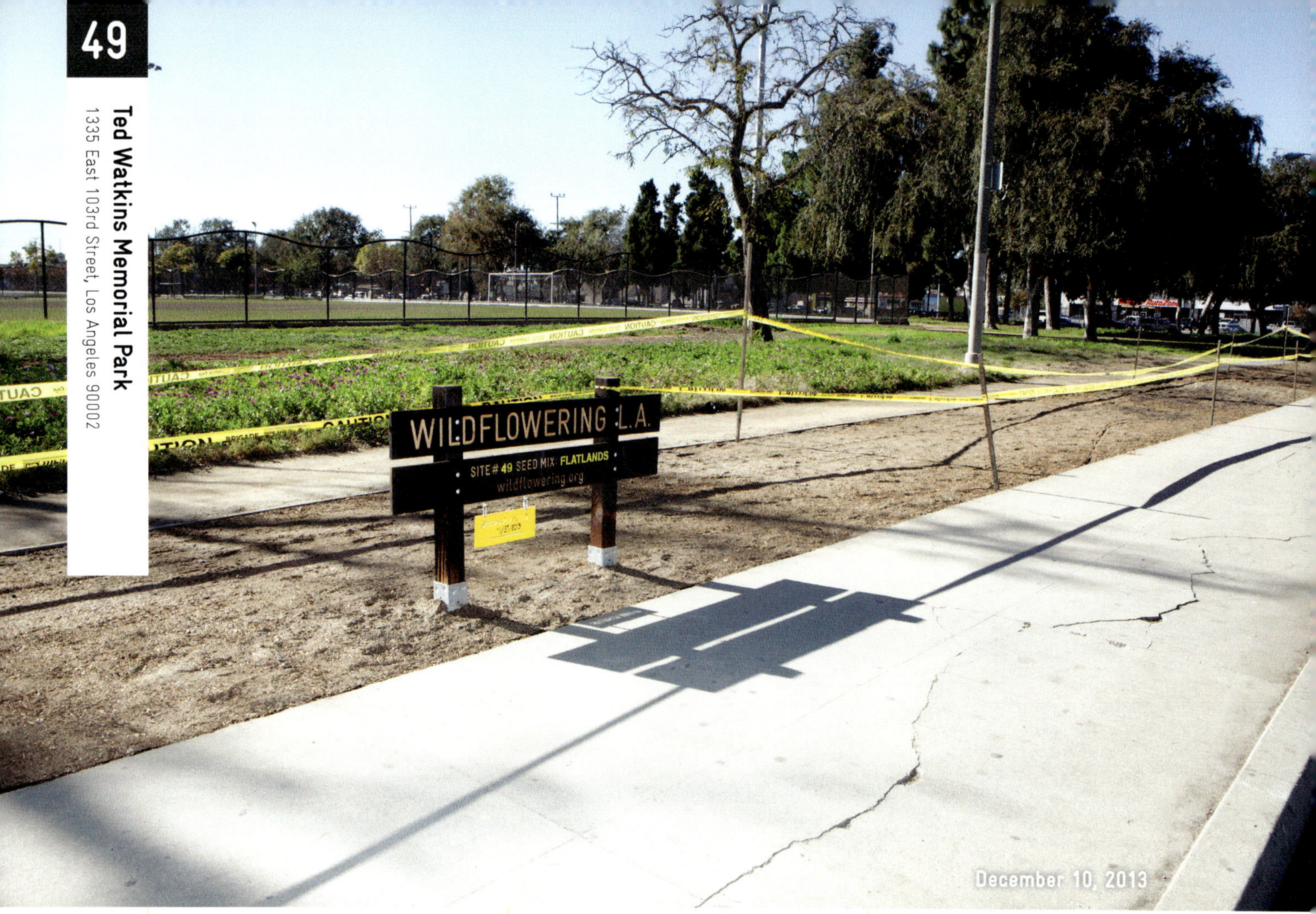

Ted Watkins Memorial Park
1335 East 103rd Street, Los Angeles 90002

DEC 12 We have completed the soil preparation and sowing of the seeds at Watkins Park in the existing planter beds divided by a decomposed walking path. Thank you for this opportunity to improve our parks.

MAR 10 We will obtain more seeds to fill in the bare areas of both of our county sites (Watkins Park and Roosevelt Park). We are expecting to be in full bloom sometime beginning of April.

MAY 14 Our sites do have some flowers, but are mainly drying and setting seed.

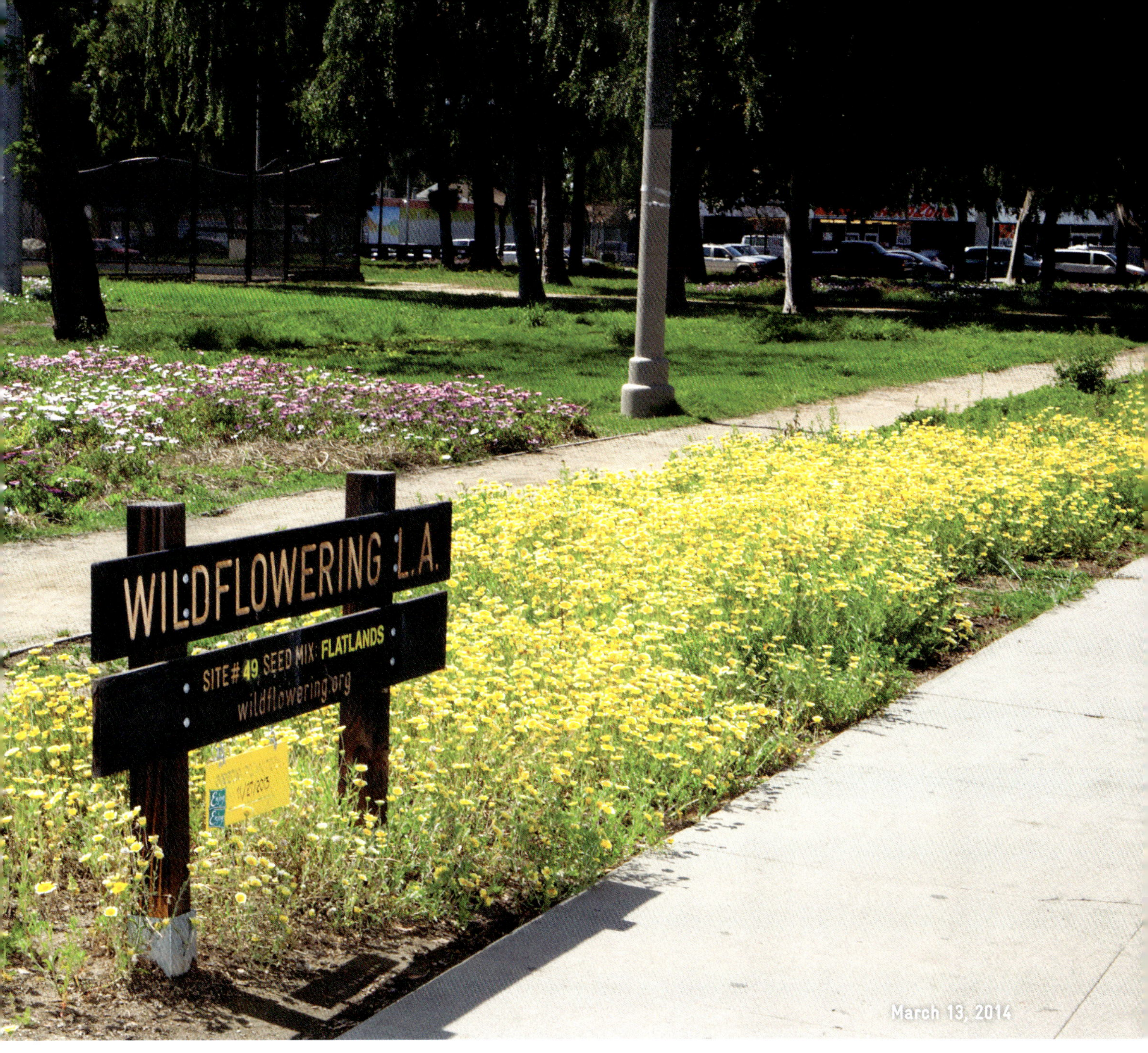

Planted by the Los Angeles County Department of Parks and Recreation staff.

Letting Wildflowers Take Over My Front Lawn

It is early July. As I look through my front window, I can see what's left of the spring blooms that only months ago covered our front yard. The tall dried stems of wildflowers cling stubbornly to the parched soil. Dotted here and there are orange poppies, which are inexplicably thriving in the heat, and the long legs of a few tenacious pink Elegant Clarkia rise from the sea of hay. I'm reminded of hikes in the Santa Monica Mountains, camping in the Sierras, and old postcards from the '70s of a girl walking in a field, the sunlight glinting in her hair. A bit of old California has been growing in our yard.

A little over two months ago, the flowers were at their peak and swaying in the breeze: bright yellow Tidy Tips; purple, pink, and white Clarkia; and tiny cornflower-blue Bird's-Eye Gilia. Bright sunlight reflected a rainbow of colors through our living room window like nature's spin art. Bees and butterflies converged on the yard, eating hungrily from the blooms, and birds danced on the stems and rummaged in the dirt for bugs.

All of this happened in my yard because of *Wildflowering L.A.*, a unique living work of art that grew in fifty locations across Los Angeles County this spring. *Wildflowering L.A.* — a project encompassing art, nature, and community-building — was masterminded by artist Fritz Haeg, who worked with the Theodore Payne Foundation for Wild Flowers and Native Plants and the curatorial non-profit LAND (Los Angeles Nomadic Division).

I learned about the project last fall when I happened to pass a stall at the Hollywood Farmers' Market. A postcard caught my eye, and I stopped to find out more. I learned that anyone could participate as long as you had a yard that was visible from the street.

My husband and I had just bought a house in Lincoln Heights that needed a lot of work. We'd planned on eventually taking out the 40-year-old

thatched grass clinging stubbornly to the ground around our house; it just
wasn't at the top of our list.

Wildflowering L.A. seemed like a perfect opportunity to expedite
removal of the eyesore that was our front lawn. It would also allow us to take
advantage of the Los Angeles Department of Water and Power's Turf Removal
Rebate, with which L.A. County residents can receive $3 per square foot to
replace their lawns with drought-tolerant landscaping.

So we submitted photos and a description of our yard, and a few
weeks later, I received an e-mail welcoming us to the program. We attended
a workshop where a group of folks from the Theodore Payne Foundation
handed out bags of seed mix and explained the planting technique
(no fertilizer or mulch; spread the seed evenly but don't dig in; water regu-
larly until the plants are established). We received the Flatlands Mix based
on the micro-climate and elevation of our yard.

A landscaping consultant informed us that our lawn was Kikuyu Grass,
which would be very difficult to remove. He was right, of course. Removing
the grass involved renting a very large sod-cutting machine that didn't
even make a dent in the lawn. When that didn't work, we had our contrac-
tors hire a few guys to dig it out with pickaxes over the better part of a hot
November weekend.

With the yard finally cleared, we sprinkled the seed, watered, and waited.
A team came by with a beautiful sign made especially for *Wildflowering L.A.*
that included our number (Site #44) and the specialized seed mix (Flatlands)
we had planted.

Our bare dirt yard with its sign resembling the kind you see in a National
Park was a curious sight. Neighbors stopped to ask: "Was the sign put
there by the city?", "What will you be growing?", and "Why did you take out
the lawn?" Some people seemed a bit disappointed that we had removed
a perfectly good lawn, so carefully tended for many years by the house's
well-loved previous owners. But they brightened when we explained what
would be growing in its place.

It felt great to engage with people face-to-face, and to have a reason to meet and talk to our new neighbors. And over the course of the dry winter, as dirt gave way to a lush meadow, our yard became a destination. On many occasions, we looked out the window to see kids looking at our yard and the description of the flowers in our seed mix, which we had laminated and hung on our fence. Neighbors who were previously skeptical waved and nodded their approval. In fact, whenever people stopped at our gate, we invited them in. It was lovely to see the smiles on their faces, and their reactions both to our hospitality and to the abundant flora and fauna.

To build a wider community, we were encouraged to tweet photos and commentary with the hashtag #wildfloweringla. A neighbor we haven't met tweeted a photo of our yard and wrote: "This house makes me so happy whenever I pass by."

Mornings brought our own personal nature show, viewed with coffee cup in hand through the large picture window. In the late afternoons, golden sunsets set the yard aglow. As the flowers began to grow, colorful birds flocked to the yard, perching on the fence and stems, rolling in the dirt, and feasting on the plentiful insects that found an enticing habitat among the nascent plant life. Multitudes of bees and butterflies happily drank nectar from the upturned yellow Tidy Tips.

Photographers came by to capture this unique site, and we were even visited one evening by non-profit organization de LaB (design east of La Brea), who organized a public tour to experience the flowers at their peak and learn about the project.

In April, there was a culminating *Wildflowering L.A.* event in which all the project participants brought cuttings from their sites and placed them on a giant map created with masking tape by artist Fritz Haeg. It was interesting to compare our experience with that of others — we bonded over what grew and what didn't, and over how much weeding and watering we had to do. Many of us came away with a feeling of camaraderie in having been part of this experiment.

A few weeks ago, a representative from *Wildflowering L.A.* came to take away the sign; we had him take one last picture of us with it in our scraggly and fawn-colored yard. We were sad to see it go. The few flowers that are still miraculously blooming from the scorched earth are proof that native plants can hold their own in this dry climate.

Now that there is a seed bank dormant in the soil of our yard, many flowers will return next spring as long as there's a bit of winter rain. In the meantime, to augment the wildflowers, we're planning a perennial California native garden that will include salvia, buckwheat, and possibly even an oak tree. Perhaps then we'll have done our part to revive a bit of old California in our neighborhood.

This piece originally appeared at Zócalo Public Square on July 16, 2014

Jennifer Mandel
Site #44

Lupinus succulentus (Arroyo Lupine)

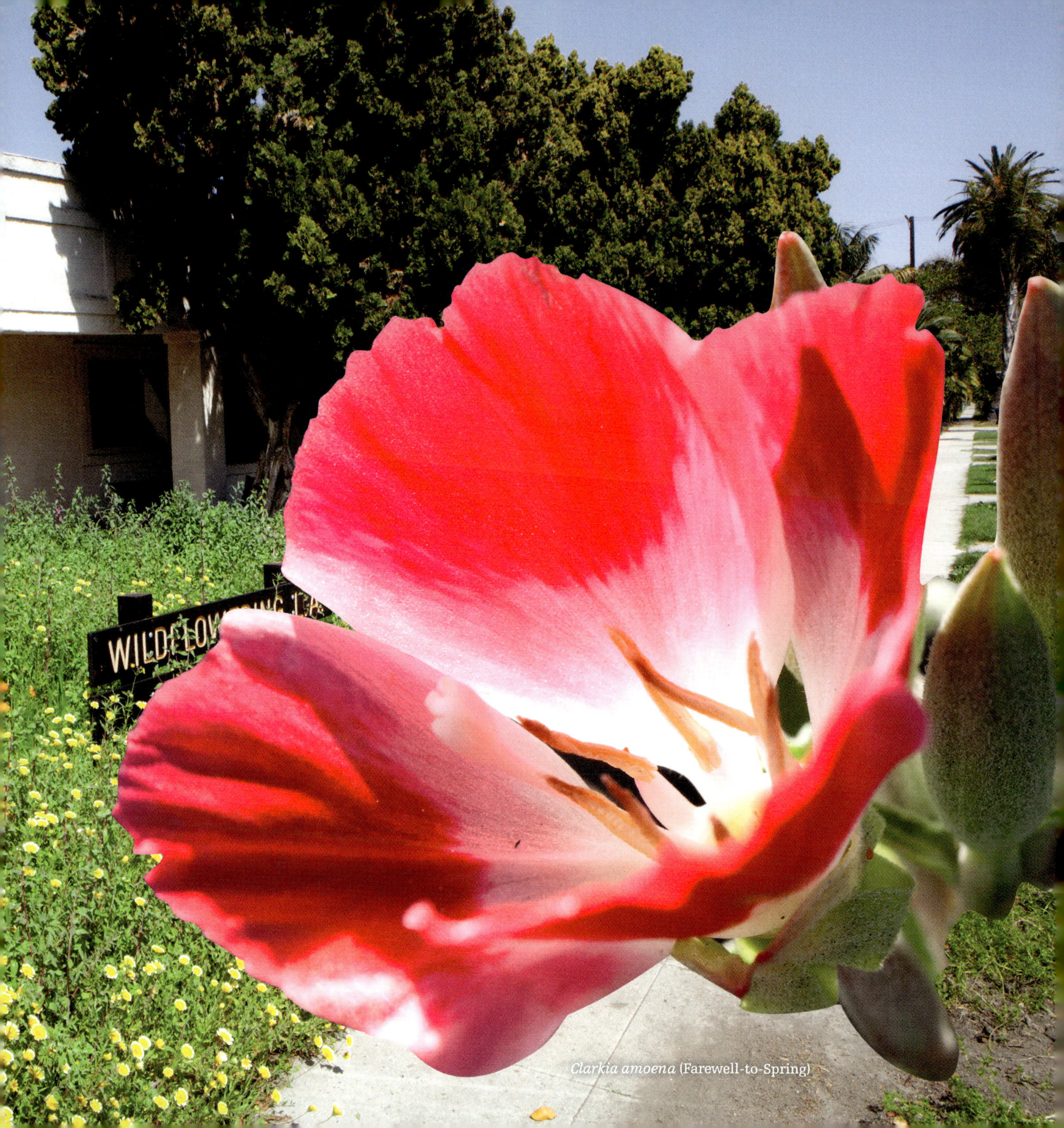

Clarkia amoena (Farewell-to-Spring)

#01 2625 Adelbert Ave
Los Angeles 90039
Hillside Mix

#02 4126 Edenhurst Ave
Los Angeles 90039
Flatlands Mix

#03 Eagle Rock
Elementary School
4900 block of
Maywood Ave
Los Angeles 90041
Flatlands Mix

#04 3132 Isabel Dr
Los Angeles 90065
Hillside Mix

#05 Arlington Garden
275 Arlington Dr
Pasadena 91105
Roadside Mix

#06 1701 Winmar Dr
Los Angeles 90065
Hillside Mix

#07 2415 N Yorkshire Dr
Los Angeles 90065
(on downslope at the
end of street)
Hillside Mix

#08 South Coast
Botanic Garden
26300 Crenshaw Blvd
Palos Verdes
Peninsula 90274
Coastal Mix

#09 20575 Cheney Dr
Topanga Canyon
90290
Hillside Mix

#10 2851 Orange Ave
La Crescenta 91214
Hillside Mix

#11 4527 Otay Dr
Los Angeles 90065
Hillside Mix

#12 3115 Cazador St
Los Angeles 90065
Hillside Mix

#13 Westridge School
324 Madeline Dr
Pasadena 91105
Flatlands Mix

#14 Pasadena Casting
Pond, Arroyo Seco
Natural Park
415 S Arroyo Blvd
Pasadena 91105
Roadside Mix

#15 N San Gabriel
Canyon Road
(Highway 39) and
Sierra Madre Ave
Azusa 91702
Roadside Mix

#16 Highland Hall
Waldorf School
17100 Superior St
Northridge 91325
Flatlands Mix

#17 1150 W Grovecenter St
Covina 91722
Flatlands Mix

#18 Fenwick St and
Olive Grove Ave
Sunland 91040
Hillside Mix

#19 1855 Park Dr
Los Angeles 90026
Hillside Mix

#20 1456 Holbrook St
Los Angeles 90041
Hillside Mix

#21 Theodore Payne
Foundation
10459 Tuxford St
Sun Valley 91352
Hillside Mix

#22 Los Angeles County
Arboretum and
Botanic Garden
301 N Baldwin Ave
Arcadia 91007
Flatlands Mix

#23 356 Mission/
Ooga Booga
356 S Mission Rd
Los Angeles 90033
Roadside Mix

#24 436 Mt Washington Dr
Los Angeles 90065
Hillside Mix

#25 2821 West View St
Los Angeles 90016
Flatlands Mix

#26 Griffith Park Blvd
and Lyric Ave
Los Angeles 90039
Hillside Mix

#27 4237 Eagle Rock Blvd
Los Angeles 90065
Roadside Mix

#28 3847 DuRay Place
Los Angeles 90008
Flatlands Mix

#29 22321 Osage Court
Torrance 90505
Coastal Mix

#30 5605 Bushnell Way
Los Angeles 90042
Hillside Mix

#31 2932 & 2934
S Harcourt Ave
Los Angeles 90016
Flatlands Mix

#32 Sage Hill
UCLA Campus
Bellagio Dr and
Sunset Blvd
Los Angeles 90095
Hillside Mix

#33 850 Laguna Ave
Los Angeles 90026
Hillside Mix

#34 3211 Minneapolis St
Los Angeles 90039
Flatlands Mix

#35 4015 San Rafael Ave
Los Angeles 90065
Hillside Mix

#36 Outback Preserve
Pitzer College
1050 N Mills Ave
Claremont 91711
Flatlands Mix

#37 College of Environ-
mental Design
Cal Poly Pomona
3801 W Temple Ave
Pomona 91768
Roadside Mix

#38 4221 & 4225 York Blvd
Los Angeles 90065
Hillside Mix

#39 10148 W Ave I
Lancaster 93536
Roadside Mix

#40 Carthay Center
Elementary School
6351 W Olympic Blvd
Los Angeles 90048
Roadside Mix

#41 8832 Villanova Ave
Los Angeles 90045
Coastal Mix

#42 5430 Sanchez Dr
Los Angeles 90008
Hillside Mix

#43 Diamond Bar United
Church of Christ
2335 S Diamond Bar Blvd
Diamond Bar 91765
Hillside Mix

#44 478 E Ave 28
Los Angeles 90031
Flatlands Mix

#45 Art Center College
of Design
1700 Lida St
Pasadena 91103
Hillside Mix

#46 Poppy Peak
6255 Annan Way
Los Angeles 90042
Hillside Mix

#47 Eagle Rock Post Office
7435 N Figueroa St
Los Angeles 90041
Flatlands Mix

#48 3940 Barryknoll Dr
Los Angeles 90065
Hillside Mix

#49 Ted Watkins
Memorial Park
1335 East 103rd St
Los Angeles 90002
Flatlands Mix

#50 Franklin D. Roosevelt Park
7600 Graham Ave
Los Angeles 90001
Flatlands Mix

LIST OF ALL PARTICIPANTS

356 Mission, Sara Abed, Leigh Adams, Carolyn Gray Anderson, Arlington Garden, Beth Armstrong-Shikano, Art Center College of Design, Lisa Anne Auerbach, Chris Barber, Marco Barrantes, Nitza Bernard, M. Charles Bernstein, Enci Box, Stephen Box, Sydney Box, Gregg Cahill, Cal Poly Pomona College of Environmental Design, Louisa Cardenas, Carthay Center Elementary School, Alex Castellon, City of Pasadena Office of the Mayor, Joe Clements, Los Angeles County Department of Parks and Recreation, IxChel Cruz-Gonzalez, Teresa Dahl, Frank deBourbon, Elizabeth Ford deBourbon, Dean Decent, Joe de Marie, Tim DeRoche, Diamond Bar United Church of Christ, Abby Diamond, Doris Duval, Eagle Rock Elementary School, Eagle Rock Neighborhood Council, Paul Faulstich, Jayme Filippini, Michelle Frier, Marjory Garrison, Matt Geldin, Elizabeth Gerber, Carrick Moore Gerrety, Tom Gillespie, Brooke Glazer, Patricia Gonzales, Emily Green, Scott M.B. Gustafson, Betsy Haffner, Sarah Halterman, Kendis Heffley, August Henrici, Highland Hall Waldorf School, Mark Infusino, Jeremy Jarin, Karly Katona, Bridget Kelley, Bob King, Roger Klemm, La Loma Development Company, John Latsko, Susan Lawrence, Stephanie Leach, Peter Liao, Jay Lieske, Joshua Link, LocalConstruct, Johann Lockard, Melissa Lockard, Los Angeles County Arboretum and Botanic Garden, Vinh X. Luong, Casey Lynch, Gail Mackenzie-Smith, William Mackenzie-Smith, Jennifer Mandel, Michelle Matthews, Lauren McCabe, Taylor McCleery, Betty McKenney, Kicker McKenney, Tom McKenzie, Maggie Miller, Amanda Millet, Monrovia Unified School District Adult Transition Program, Timothy Nolan, Diana Offen, Faith Oftadeh, Ade Onaolapo, Margot Ott, Ian Page, Pasadena Casting Club, Julia Paull, Michael Paynca, Madelyn Payne, Ernesto Perez, Michael Pigneguy, Pitzer College, Michelle Ramage, Brendan Ravenhill, Chelsea Robinson, The Rosato Family, Corey Rovzar, Pedra Sage, Jude Schwendenwien, Richard Schulhof, Izzy Sherman, Lily Sherman, Yohei Shikano, Fontelle Slater, South Coast Botanic Garden, Don Sticksel, Rhonda Stone, Jean Sudbury, Christy Sumner, Shya Sumner, Ethan Swan, Steven Synstelien, Ted Tegart, Tiffanie Tran, Chris Tufty, University of California Los Angeles, Miguel Vasquez, Shannon Waddell, Timothy Wager, Pamela Wagner, Westridge Community Service Action Group (Grade 7), Westridge School, Andrew O. Wilcox, Simon Wilkinson, Brian Williams, Julie Williams, Mika Yamamoto, Wendy Yao, Melissa Zimmermann

LAND (LOS ANGELES NOMADIC DIVISION)

LAND (Los Angeles Nomadic Division) is a non-profit organization founded in 2009 committed to curating site-specific public art exhibitions in Los Angeles and beyond. LAND believes that everyone deserves the opportunity to experience innovative contemporary art in their day-to-day lives. In turn, artists deserve the opportunity to realize projects, otherwise unsupported, at unique sites in the public realm.

FRITZ HAEG

Fritz Haeg is an artist whose work has included edible gardens, public dances, educational environments, animal architecture, domestic gatherings, urban parades, temporary encampments, documentary videos, publications, exhibitions, and occasionally buildings for people. Haeg is a 2010–11 Rome Prize Fellow and has taught architecture, design, and fine art programs at universities and colleges across the country. Haeg has produced projects and exhibited work at the Tate Modern, the Hayward Gallery, the Liverpool Biennial, MoMA, the Whitney Museum of American Art, SFMOMA, SALT Beyoğlu (Istanbul), and Casco (Utrecht), among many other notable institutions nationally and internationally.

Wildflowering L.A. is a project by artist Fritz Haeg

Curated and presented by LAND
(Los Angeles Nomadic Division)

Wildflower consulting by the Theodore Payne Foundation for
Wild Flowers and Native Plants

Graphic design and identity by Roman Jaster

Sign fabrication by Knowhow Shop

Photography by Isabel Avila

Supported by a grant from The James Irvine Foundation's
Exploring Engagement Fund

wildflowering.org

Published by LAND (Los Angeles Nomadic Division).

ISBN 978-0-9827575-2-9

Executive Publisher/Editor: LAND/Shamim M. Momin

Editors: Samantha Frank and Maryam Hosseinzadeh

Book Design: Yay Brigade (Roman Jaster and Nicole Jaffe)

This book is distributed by
LAND (Los Angeles Nomadic Division)
8033 Sunset Boulevard #455
Los Angeles, CA 90046
www.nomadicdivision.org

Printed in Las Vegas Nevada by Creel
2015

CREDITS

Quote on pp. 4–5: Payne, Theodore. *Theodore Payne in His Own Words: A Voice for California Native Plants.* Pasadena: Many Moons Press, 2004. Print.

Special thanks to Leigh Adams, Genevieve Arnold, Reyner Banham, Laurice Becker, Sima Bernstein, Cal Poly Pomona College of Environmental Design, Richard Carlos, Kitty Connolly, deLaB, Steve Gerischer, Lynette Kampe, Karly Katona, KCHUNG, La Loma Development Company/The Shed, Joan M. Leong, Los Angeles County Arboretum and Botanic Garden, Los Angeles County Arts Commission, Los Angeles County Second Supervisorial District, Los Angeles River Revitalization Corporation, Ryan Maxey, MOCAtv, Otis College of Art and Design Graduate Public Practice Program, Josh Polon, Rancho Cienega Recreation Center, Richard Schulhof, Lili Singer, Steve Singer, Sustainable Economic Enterprises of Los Angeles, and Zócalo Public Square.

LAND Staff: Shamim M. Momin, Director and Curator; Laura Hyatt, Associate Director; Samantha Frank, Director of Exhibitions/ Curatorial Manager; Maryam Hosseinzadeh, Project Coordinator, *Wildflowering L.A.*; Jennie Waldow, Administrative and Research Assistant; Jamie Costa, Development Assistant

LAND Board of Directors: Thao Nguyen, President; Lori DeWolfe, Treasurer; Stephen Maguire; Kelsey Lee Offield; John Yoon; Shamim M. Momin, Acting Secretary

Front Cover: *Wildflowering L.A.* site #44. Photo by Isabel Avila.

Back Cover: *Wildflowering L.A.* site #50. Photo by Isabel Avila.

Page 1: Los Angeles County map of *Wildflowering L.A.* sites

Page 68: Detail of Northeast Los Angeles site map

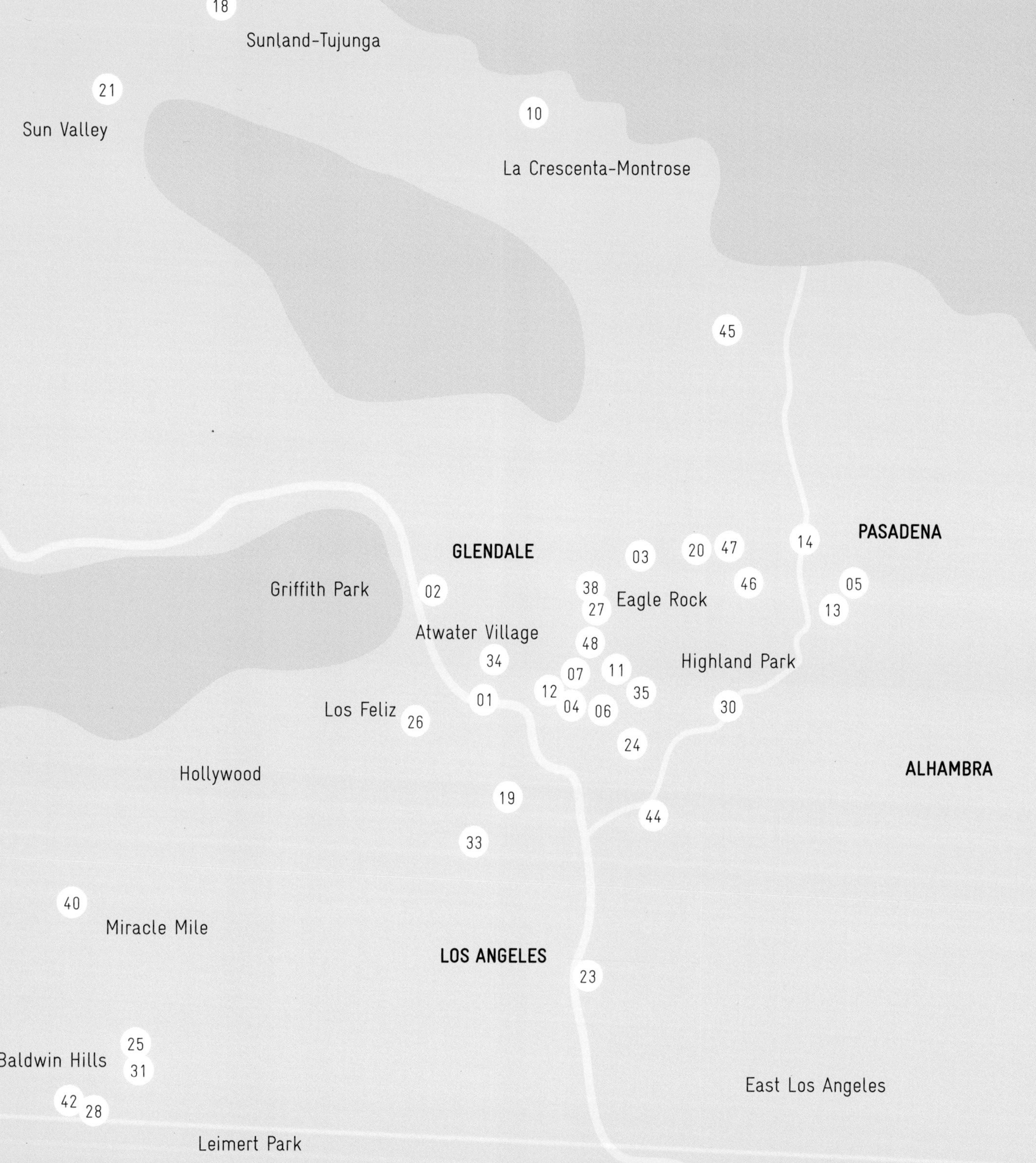

18
Sunland-Tujunga
21
Sun Valley
10
La Crescenta-Montrose
45
GLENDALE
03
20
47
14
PASADENA
Griffith Park
02
38
Eagle Rock
27
46
05
13
Atwater Village
48
Highland Park
34
07
11
01
12
35
Los Feliz
04
06
26
30
24
Hollywood
ALHAMBRA
19
44
33
40
Miracle Mile
LOS ANGELES
23
25
Baldwin Hills
31
East Los Angeles
42
28
Leimert Park